Ask COSMO girl!

About Your Body

**All the Answers to Your Most
Intimate Questions**

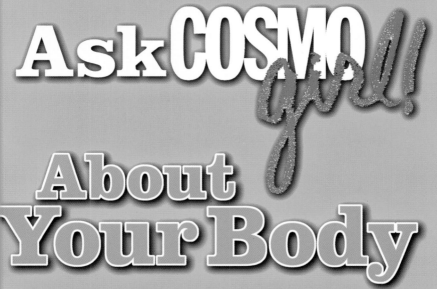

Ask COSMO girl!

About Your Body

All the Answers to Your Most Intimate Questions

From The Editors of CosmoGIRL!

Hearst Books
A Division of Sterling Publishing Co., Inc.
New York

Library of Congress Cataloging-in-Publication Data

Ask Cosmogirl! about your body : all the answers to your most intimate questions / from the editors of CosmoGIRL.
    p. cm.
 Includes index.
 ISBN 1-58816-486-1
 1. Teenage girls—Health and hygiene—Juvenile literature. 2. Teenage girls—Health and hygiene—Miscellanea. I. Title: Ask Cosmo girl! about your body. II. Cosmo girl.

  RA777.25.A85 2006
  613'.04243—dc22

2005013052

10 9 8 7 6 5 4 3 2

Book design by Margaret Rubiano

CosmoGIRL! and Hearst Books are trademarks of Hearst Communications, Inc.

www.cosmogirl.com

For information about custom editions, special sales, premium and corporate purchases, please contact Sterling Special Sales Department at 800-805-5489 or specialsales@sterlingpub.com.

Distributed in Canada by Sterling Publishing
$^c/_o$ Canadian Manda Group, 165 Dufferin Street
Toronto, Ontario, Canada M6K 3H6

Distributed in Australia by Capricorn Link (Australia) Pty. Ltd.
P.O. Box 704, Windsor, NSW 2756 Australia

Printed in China

Sterling ISBN 13: 978-1-58816-486-5
      ISBN 10: 1-58816-486-1

Photo credits: Brooke Nipar, pg. 92; Coliena Rentmeester, pg. 120; Saye, pg. 54, 78; Michael Wirth, pg. 10.

CoNTEnTs

FOREWORD

From Me to You

Your body. Isn't it the weirdest thing? You own it, you're in charge of it, you've lived in it for your entire life. But there are so many things about your body that you just don't understand. You assume you're growing the way you're supposed to, but it can be kind of unsettling to not really know for sure. That's why you come to CosmoGIRL! with tons of questions about your body—it's only in the past few years that you've been paying attention to how it works and the changes that go on day to day, month to month, year to year, so it's normal that you'd suddenly have an onslaught of "Why does...? What is...? What the????!!!" questions. But the fact that you have all of these questions is actually a great thing, because it means you're curious and you want to know that you're normal and healthy and how to stay that way. We totally support that, which is why we started our Body & Soul section in CosmoGIRL!—to give you all kinds of information on your health, physically, mentally, and emotionally. And here, in this book, we've compiled the answers to all of your most important, most intimate, and in some cases most embarrassing body questions. We know it can be hard to ask your mom or even your doctor these things. Not that you should ever feel ashamed to ask them—it's one of the reasons they're there!—but when you just can't quite bring yourself to go to them to ask about hairy nipples, smelly discharge, or, um, gas problems, that's where CG! comes in! You can always ask us anything, and we'll tell you the honest truth, so that you can take good care of yourself today and into the future. A healthy CosmoGIRL! is a happy CosmoGIRL!, right? And when your body's fit and functioning, that's when you're ready to take on the world in all the amazing ways that you do. So use this book as a resource and keep those body questions coming to me at susan@cosmogirl.com. I'm here for you, CG!s!

Love,

Susan

ChAPTeR 1

body basics

It's your body—and it doesn't come with an owner's manual. So what's up with all the wacky things that go on with it? And how can you tell if you're normal? Guess what—everyone has body questions—and we've got answers. Read on and see if any of these sound like you!

no sweat!

Q **"I've never thought of myself as a nervous person or anything like that, but my hands sweat so much that sometimes, sweat actually drips off them. It's so gross, I can't imagine holding hands with my boyfriend—or even shaking anyone's hand ever! What should I do about it?"**

A Everyone gets sweaty hands sometimes, but our medical experts tell us that having sweat literally drip off your hands is kind of unusual—especially if it's happening all the time. You might have a rare hereditary condition known as hyperhidrosis, which causes the nerves that control perspiration to overreact. People with hyperhidrosis (1 percent of the population has it) sweat from their hands, armpits, or even their faces—even when it's not hot, and they're not nervous or overexerting themselves. It isn't a serious medical problem, but we understand why you'd rather be less drippy!

There are two anti-sweat remedies that can sometimes tame hyperhidrosis. Try sprinkling some baby powder on your palms throughout the day or rolling on Certain Dri (a super-strong anti-perspirant you can get at a drug store). If those quick fixes don't work, schedule an appointment with your doctor. Tell her your *exact* sweat symptoms so she knows that you're suffering from around-the-clock wetness, and not just occasional sweat associated with exercise or nervousness. She'll make sure hyperhidrosis is the cause, then she'll probably prescribe a special antiperspirant called Drysol for you to rub into your palms every night. (It plugs up your sweat glands so you won't sweat the next day.) If that doesn't work, there are other options. You can get a prescription for something called a Drionic machine which dries out your sweat glands for days, even weeks, at a time by zapping them with electricity. It costs about $125, and insurance often covers it. Or you can opt for a more permanent solution: an outpatient surgery that fixes the overactive nerves. It's pretty painless. (Really! A *CosmoGIRL!* editor just had it done!) This option can cost up to $4,500 or more, but all or most of it is usually covered by insurance. To learn more about hyperhidrosis, check out **hyperhidrosis.org**.

CG! TIP: Carry a liter bottle of water around with you at all times. If it's always around, you'll remember to drink more H_2O.

BODY BASICS

Q **"I have an embarrassing problem: I sweat a lot under my arms. Why does this happen, and what can I do to stop it from happening?"**

A The best way to stop the sweat is to use antiperspirant. Antiperspirant works like this: A little perspiration inside your sweat glands reaches the surface of your skin, mixes with the antiperspirant, dissolves, and seeps back into your sweat ducts and plugs them up. Those plugs are what prevent more sweat from reaching your skin's surface. The ideal time for those plugs to form is overnight—not in the a.m., when you're running around and possibly working up a sweat that can "wash" plugs away. See, the small, sustained amount of sweat you produce when you sleep helps form the barrier of plugs. So apply a layer of antiperspirant at night before bed. Then, in the morning, apply again as usual. You won't wash away your "shield" in the shower—it lasts until your skin sloughs off (through shaving or your skin's own renewal cycle). Apply your antiperspirant regularly so that you can continue to replace the plugs. If this doesn't work, see your dermatologist—she can prescribe a medication that works to block sweat glands.

CG! TIP: Deodorant and antiperspirant don't work as well on wet skin so be sure you dry your underarms before you apply.

hairy business

Q "I have one black, coarse hair growing out of my neck. I've pulled it out, but it keeps growing back. What is it, and how can I get it to go away?"

A That kind of hair actually has a name. It's called a "terminal hair," and having one (or several) on your neck or chin is common and totally normal. Unlike the soft fuzz that's on most of your body, terminal hairs are dark and coarser. Typically, they're found under your arms or across your pubic region (but don't freak—the hair on your neck is not a pubic hair!). Occasionally, though, a regular hair follicle will just spontaneously morph into a terminal follicle. And that appears to be what you've got. If you really want to lose it for good, then you've got two options. The first is electrolysis, which uses an electric current to destroy the hair follicle. It can work well if, as in your case, you're only getting rid of one hair. But there is a risk of scarring. To find a licensed electrologist, log onto **electrology.com** (a half hour treatment costs around $35–$45). The second method, laser hair removal, shouldn't cause scarring but costs a hefty $75–$100 per session in a dermatologist's office. (Neither procedure guarantees permanent results and several treatments may be needed.) A dermatologist can tell you which procedure is better for you. To find a dermatologist, go to the American Academy of Dermatology Web site at **aad.org**. But it's one hair—so you might want to take the time to pluck it out once a month.

BODY BASICS

Q "I lose a lot of hair in the shower, and more when I blow-dry. Could I be going bald?"

A You're probably not balding. Everyone loses about 70 to 120 hairs a day, but you have around 175,000 to begin with, so that's not a lot. And we molt (yup, like birds!) twice a year, shedding a ton more! No, you won't see a bald spot—there are hairs growing in where the others fell out. Some experts believe clogged scalp follicles cause hair to fall out, so if this is a concern of yours, wash your hair weekly with an exfoliating cleanser to unclog them. If you're losing way more than 100 hairs a day, or if you do find a bald spot, it could be hormonal—see your doctor.

CG! TIP: If you get red skin after waxing, don't use products with glycolic or salicyclic acid a week before waxing and don't exfoliate that day or the day before.

what a pain!

Q "I get a lot of headaches. Mostly, they're not so bad, so I just pop some Advil and get on with my day. I just worry that I get so many of them. Could something be seriously wrong with me?

A Over-the-counter painkillers, such as acetaminophen (like Tylenol) or ibuprofen (like Nuprin), provide temporary relief. But if those painkillers are used too often, your body's natural pain-fighting ability actually gets weaker. The result: a nasty "rebound" headache that comes back even stronger. This might be what's happening to you, so limit yourself to four pills a day over a couple of days. If your headaches continue, be sure to see a doctor to rule out anything more serious that may be causing them.

CG! TIP: Sometimes headaches can be brought on by bad posture. When you're sitting, don't hunch over. Keep both feel flat on the floor and sit with your back upright.

BODY BaSiCs

Q **"I keep getting these annoying mouth ulcers. What causes them— and how can I stop getting them?"**

A Mouth ulcers (or canker sores) are tiny, whitish-red craters that crop up on the tongue, gums, or inside the cheek. These sores are often so tender that it's hard to eat without major pain. But they're not dangerous or anything—and with proper care, you can try to prevent them. Here's how: cut back on canker-causing foods. Sugary foods, citrus fruits, and coffee are all suspected to bring on cankers. Also, brushing your teeth too hard can spark a sore, so brush lightly with a soft-bristle brush to avoid irritating your gums. Some antiseptic mouthwashes and tartar-control toothpastes contain chemicals that can irritate the lining of the mouth, causing a sore. Ditching the harsh mouthwash and using an all-natural toothpaste (with fluoride!) may do the trick. Food-wise, not getting enough nutrients—especially folic acid, iron, and vitamin B_{12}—can also cause canker sores. Get your recommended dietary allowances of these nutrients daily. Try eating a bowl of fortified cereal (like Total) for breakfast, and a sandwich made with whole-wheat bread for lunch. Now, if none of these suggestions work, you could try an over-the-counter medicine, like Oragel. It will make the canker *feel* better by numbing the surrounding nerves. Home remedies, such as hot tea, can also lessen pain. If you get canker sores really often, see a dentist. She can prescribe a steroid cream to ease the pain.

Q "I've been noticing random bruises all over my body. They just seem to appear for no reason at all. Could there be something wrong with me?"

A You've probably heard rumors that a lack of muscle tone or not enough vitamin C can make you bruise more easily, but that's not true. Bruises are wounds under your skin that usually occur when you hurt yourself and the blood escapes from the vessels into the tissues of your skin. The blood doesn't get released through your skin (like it does when you get a cut); it just pools below the surface layer of your skin, causing discoloration. Not to call you klutzy, but the most likely scenario is that you're just bumping into things without realizing it, and that's what's causing your bruises. Another possible cause: Do you take aspirin regularly? Even one dose a day can make it harder for your blood to clot, which makes it easier for you to bruise. But just so we give you *all* the facts, there is a *tiny* possibility that the bruises you are experiencing are a sign of a more serious medical condition (less than 2 percent of people bruise without having some kind of trauma to their skin). If you just started getting the bruises and they're continuing or getting worse, and if you feel tired or weak or have very heavy periods and gums that bleed when you brush your teeth, see a doctor ASAP for blood testing. It could possibly be a sign of leukemia, or a hereditary condition like blood-clotting or connective-tissue dysfunction. If these are left undiagnosed, they can be dangerous. To ease your mind, tell your doctor about your bruises on your next visit to her office so that she can make sure everything checks out.

will it leave a mark?

Q "I recently got a bad burn on my leg, and I'm afraid it's going to scar. How can I stop that from happening?"

A If it's not blistering and feels like a sunburn, you can treat it on your own. (If it is blistering, or if the skin is loose, go to a doctor. It's likely a deeper second- or third-degree burn, which needs special care.) Now, despite what you may have heard, you should never put butter on a burn—it acts as food for bacteria (and bacteria can cause infection, which can lead to scarring). Instead, immediately run cold water over the burn for at least 30 minutes. This will reduce swelling and skin trauma, which minimizes the risk of scarring. Applying an antibiotic ointment like Bacitracin will also help prevent infection. Cover the burn loosely with gauze once a day or whenever it gets wet. Now, if the scab peels...no picking! Picking can cause (you guessed it!) scarring. If you think you have an infection (symptoms include red streaks, swelling, pus, odor, or fever), go to your doctor right away—you need an antibiotic.

Once the wound has completely healed (there's no more scab and it's completely dry), start using a vitamin E cream or cocoa butter twice a day. And, from now on, put sunscreen on the area (SPF 30 or higher). Skin that's been badly burned can be more sensitive to the sun.

Q **"I always get scars on my legs from mosquito bites. How can I get rid of them?"**

A Dab a cream that's 2 percent hydroquinone, a skin-lightening ingredient, over the spots twice a day for three months or until they've faded. To hide the marks, apply one or two coats of a spray foundation all over your legs and rub it in like body lotion. Try not to scratch those bites! Scratching equals scarring. To curb the urge, put ice on fresh bites for five minutes to stop the release of histamine, which causes the itching, then apply a 1 percent cortisone cream.

Q **"I was with my boyfriend last night and he left me something my parents are not going to like very much: a big purple hickey! How can I get rid of it before they see it?!"**

A A hickey is basically a bruise, so to make it go away, treat it just like you would a bruise. Coat the hickey with aloe vera, then rub it in with the back of a frozen spoon (we're not kidding—always keep a spoon in the freezer!) for 10 minutes daily to speed fading. The icy spoon helps constrict blood vessels, so there's less bleeding under the skin; the aloe will help reduce inflammation.

BODY BASICS

foot fixes

Q "I have itchy feet all the time. I've noticed also that my toenails are yellow. It's so gross. What should I do?"

A Sounds to us like a case of athlete's foot. A good natural remedy to soothe the annoying itching—believe it or not—is raw garlic! The oils from raw, fresh garlic will reduce the itch and may even help kill the fungus. Take one clove of garlic and cut it in half. Rub the garlic over the infected areas of your foot, between and around your toes. Leave the juices on for 30 minutes, then rinse with warm water and dry thoroughly. Do this once a day for a week. In the meantime, while you're healing, always dry in between your toes after showering and change your socks at least once a day. Also, avoid wearing the same pair of shoes every day. You want to give your shoes a little more time than that to "air out" before wearing them. If the garlic remedy doesn't work—or if you're not willing to rub garlic all over your feet!—there are lots of over-the-counter remedies for athlete's foot, including Lamisil-AT, Desenex (undecylenic acid), Lotrimin (clotrimazole), Monistat-Derm (miconazole), and Tinactin (tolnaftate), all of which take four weeks to get rid of the itchy foot fungus.

CG! TIP: When applying scrubs and moisture treatments onto your body, always use long, brisk strokes, which stimulate circulation and give your skin a pretty glow.

Q "I can't take off my shoes because my feet smell horrible. What can I do?"

A You may have bromidrosis, a disorder you can get if your feet sweat a lot. What happens is, bacteria live off your sweat and cause an odor. But if you have an odor plus a rash on your feet or discolored nails, it's probably a fungal infection. Either way, podiatrists suggest you wash your feet with an antibacterial soap in the a.m. and spray an antiperspirant (the kind used for underarms) on your toes and feet. At night, wash them again. If it's fungal, apply an antifungal cream like Lamisil as the last step. And if your shoes smell, the bacterial or fungal infection lives there too, so throw them in the washer and spray them twice daily with an antifungal spray, like Micatin. Want a natural way to make your tootsies smell better? Make a foot bath by adding one tablespoon of grapefruit juice to one quart of water and boil 10 minutes. Add cold water till it's a comfortable temperature. Soak your feet 20 minutes, then pat dry. If odor persists, repeat daily till it's gone. Within two weeks, your feet and shoes should be infection-free. But if you're still smelly, see a podiatrist.

CG! TIP: Sprinkle the inside of your shoes with dried sage. Sage is really potent and fresh-smelling—a great cover-up!

stinky situations!

Q "I have really bad breath and would like to try a natural remedy to cure it. What can you recommend?"

A Bacteria thrive on food stuck in your mouth and this can cause bad breath. That said, the main way to get rid of bad breath is to get rid of this trapped food. The best way to do that is to keep your teeth clean. After each meal, sprinkle one to rwo teaspoons of salt into a glass of water and swish it around in your mouth for 20 seconds; then spit. Repeat three times. The salt rinse will help remove those pesky bits of food and make your breath fresh!

CG! TIP: To naturally combat bad breath, chew on fennel, licorice, or parsley after eating. These herbs sweeten breath and mask the bad smell.

Q "I have this bad odor inside my belly button. I have tried cleaning it, but it comes back. What could it be?"

A That cute little dot is actually a tough place to keep clean, especially if you have an "innie," where dead skin cells, oil, and dirt can build up deep inside and stink up the place. So the first step is to make sure that your naval hygiene is up to snuff. Be sure to gently clean the entire area, inside and out, with an antibacterial soap every day. If there's still a smell, use a Q-tip dipped in astringent to reach the tough spots and sweep away any germs. Still stinky after a few weeks? You might have a bacterial infection. It's not hard to get one; you could've scratched and accidentally broken the skin inside your navel, allowing dirt and germs from your fingernail to enter your bloodstream. If your belly button's pierced, then your infection risk can be higher. Other signs of infection include redness, pain, even a yellowish discharge. To get rid of the infection, rub a Q-tip dipped in antibacterial ointment inside the naval area three times a day. Within a week, the smell should be back to normal. If that doesn't work, make an appointment with your doctor. A smelly belly button could also signal a yeast infection. In that case, you may need a prescription medicine to get rid of it.

peeroblems?

Q **"Whenever I laugh really hard, I start to pee my pants. How can I make it stop?"**

A You have a common condition that doctors call "giggle pees"—seriously! When you laugh, the bladder muscle gets a signal to contract, which opens the bladder "neck," letting some urine leak out. The hormone estrogen helps control bladder muscles. But between the ages of 11 and 17, estrogen levels are fluctuating, and when estrogen is low, you're less able to control the muscles that prevent you from peeing—so you end up leaking when you laugh. Once your estrogen levels become more regular, your problem should go away on its own. For now, just wear a panty liner when you think you might be laughing.

Q "Is there a reason my urine has such a strong odor to it?"

A The thing about odor is that it can signal when something's wrong—but more often, it's just the body doing its thing. Foul-smelling urine could be caused by something harmless, like drinking coffee or eating asparagus, which contain strong-smelling chemicals that become concentrated when broken down by your digestive system. It could also mean you're not drinking enough water—the less water in your urine, the stronger the odor. You can dilute it by drinking at least eight glasses of water a day (drink more if you play sports or exercise). But if your pee smells fishy—and along with the odor, you have to pee a lot or feel pain when you go—it could be a sign that you have a urinary tract infection, or UTI. This condition is very common among young women. If you have one, you'll need to see your doctor for some medicine to clear up the infection. If none of these sound like your situation and you have a clean bill of health from your doc, it's possible that your urine naturally smells that way.

CG! TIP: Are you drinking enough water? Take your weight, divide it by two, and drink that many ounces of water each day.

BoDy BaSiCs

Q "I get a lot of urinary tract infections. What can I do to prevent them from coming back all the time?"

A "Don't worry—you're not alone. Urinary tract infections affect one out of every five women! They occur when bacteria from the lower intestine colonize the bladder. To prevent UTIs, you always want to keep your genital area as clean as possible, and always wipe front to back after using the toilet, whether you pooped or not. You want to keep all that pesky bacteria away from your vaginal opening and your urethra. You can also prevent UTIs by emptying your bladder every time you pee (make sure you're completely finished before getting up). Cotton underwear breathes, and provides a less friendly environment for bacteria to breed, which makes it a healthy alternative to silk and underwear made from synthetic material, like Lycra. And you can also drink it away. Also, a study confirms that drinking 16 ounces of cranberry juice a day helps keep UTIs away. The juice's high acidity prevents bacteria from growing in the bladder.

acne solutions

Q "Help! I'm 15 years old and have been breaking out for two years! My mom keeps telling me 'it's just a phase.' How can I tell her that this is ruining my life?"

A Your mom probably knows all too well what you're going through, but as it's been years since she's gone through it herself, she may just need a gentle reminder about what it's like to be a teenager with acne. We suggest that you arrange to have a special mother-daughter chat with her to explain how you're feeling and ask her to take you to a dermatologist. Present the facts: let her know that untreated acne can cause physical scars, plus permanent damage to your self-esteem and confidence. Also, this "phase" could last well into your 30s! And don't forget to remind her how she felt when she was a teenager (chances are, if you've got acne, so did she!).

CG! TIP: Breaking out a lot? To prevent the spread of pimple-causing bacteria, try not to rest your face in your hands or press the phone up to your chin when talking on the phone.

BODY BaSiCs

workout blues

Q "I usually only have time to exercise at night, around bedtime. Is that all right?"

A Absolutely—*when* you work out has an effect on how many calories you burn or how toned your muscles become. The important thing is how regularly you work out: For best results, doctors say you should aim for at least 30 minutes of heart-raising cardio activity every day. That said, we've got two warnings about evening sweat sessions: (1) Stay safe! Use an exercise video at home or go to your local gym. If you must run outside, run with at least one buddy. (2) Late-night workouts may make you feel too revved up to sleep. If this happens to you, cool off during the last 10 minutes of your session with some gentle stretches or yoga moves.

CG! TIP: To avoid injury when working out, be sure to stretch before and after you exercise.

Q **"Whenever I run, I get really bad side cramps. Is there anything I can do to prevent them—or make them go away?"**

A The cramps are probably caused by one (or more) of the following: dehydration (not drinking enough water during the day), irregular breathing (people often forget to breathe during workouts), or overexertion (simply pushing yourself too hard). To reduce cramping, drink two glasses of water about 30 minutes before you begin your workout, and train yourself to breathe rhythmically (turn down your MP3 player so you can hear your breath). To do this, walk briskly for five minutes, then ease into your stride, matching your breath to your running rhythm (for example, inhale when you step on your right foot and exhale when you step on it again). If you still feel a cramp coming on, you're pushing too hard. Walk until the cramp subsides, and slowly increase your pace when you're ready. Or try this method: Run for 10 minutes, power walk for another 10, and so on. It's a kinder way to train your body, and over time, you'll run longer, walk less—and forget all about those annoying cramps!

CG! TIP: Alternate competitive activities, like soccer, with something like yoga. Too much adrenaline from sports can stress out your system.

BODY BASICS

Q "I get charley horses all the time—when I sleep, walk, run, and sit still. What causes them, and what can I do about them?"

A Charley horses are muscle cramps in your legs or feet. If they truly happen *all* the time—as in *every* hour—see your doctor. But if you only get them within a few hours of exercising or in the middle of the night, there are things you can do right away to stop or reduce them. Charley horses usually mean one of two things: (1) You just started a new sport and are moving and stretching your muscles in different ways, but they're too tight and not yet used to how they're being used. Instead of your muscle fibers contracting and relaxing smoothly like they usually do, they stay contracted, which can cause a cramp. (2) You're dehydrated, which means you're sweating away body fluids with minerals like sodium and potassium. Those minerals help muscles contract and relax properly, so when you lose too many of them through sweat, muscle fibers can stay in that contracted position. The result? A cramp. To prevent charley horses, always stretch your calves and feet before working out. To stay hydrated, drink water when you wake up, then a half an hour before you work out. Sip while exercising (a few gulps every 10 to 15 minutes) and afterward to replenish fluids lost through sweat. It may seem like a lot, but follow these guidelines and your cramps will be a thing of the past.

gut feelings

Q "I'm embarrassed to ask anyone for help about this, but lately I've had to fart all the time, and sometimes one slips. How can I stop?"

A You're not alone—experts say that most people fart about 15 to 20 times a day! And unfortunately, once you've brewed one up, there's not much you can do—except maybe find a crowded hallway fast! But there are ways you can cut down on cutting the cheese. (Okay, we'll stop!) First, ease up on the fiber. You say you're passing gas more than you used to—have you changed your diet to be healthier recently? We ask because, sadly, eating more healthy, high-fiber foods like vegetables and bran cereal can backfire (hee hee) gas-wise because fiber is not digestible. And while your body is struggling to break it down, it can ferment and produce gas in your intestines. So if you want to eat more veggies (and we support you!), avoid loading up on gassy greens like cabbage and broccoli. Stick with other healthy foods that have agreed with you in the past. You can also try a supplement. If you're about to eat something that you just know will give you gas (for a list of "problem" foods, check out **beanogas.com/foodlist.asp**), try a supplement like Beano, which will help you digest the food more easily.

If your diet isn't causing that embarrassing gas situation, our advice is slow down. Eating and drinking too fast, along with drinking carbonated beverages like soda, can cause you to swallow excess air along with your meal, which eventually comes back to haunt you—and everyone near you (sorry, we couldn't resist)—in the form of excess gas.

CG! TIP: Eat good fat. Healthy fats found in nuts, fish, and olive oil nourish cells and make your skin glow.

Q. "Every time I eat ice cream, I feel like my intestines are going to tear themselves right out of my stomach. What's wrong with me?"

A. If dairy seems to set you off, you (like 15 percent of your fellow Americans) might be lactose-intolerant. This means you're missing the enzyme that digests milk. Lactose intolerance can cause diarrhea, abdominal bloating, and gas. Try taking a dairy supplement like Lactaid right before you down your Ben & Jerry's to see if that helps the situation.

Q "I get gassy at night, so it freaks me out whenever I go to a sleepover. How can I stop it and save my dignity?"

A Everyone passes gas about 15 times a day (often noise-lessly). It's a byproduct of the bacteria in the colon that helps digest food. Pain occurs when stubborn gas in your intestine don't easily digest, resulting in spasms. But what you're worried about is foul-smelling gas, which is caused by high-fiber foods like broccoli, whole grains, beans, and dairy. So try avoiding these foods the day of your next sleepover. And if you don't take any other medications, try an over-the-counter charcoal tablet like CharcoCaps right before or after you eat to absorb gas. (If you're on medication, take your medi-cine two hours before or after you take CharcoCaps.) A natural way to combat gas is put a couple of drops of peppermint oil in an 8-ounce glass of water and drink up. If discomfort persists, have another glass. The menthol in the peppermint oil helps ease the spasms, controlling your discomfort.

BODY BaSiCs

Q **"I've heard that apples can help ease gastric problems. Is that really true?"**

A The expression "An apple a day keeps the doctor away" isn't really that far from the truth, especially when it comes to keeping your digestive system running smoothly. One big apple has five grams of fiber—about 25 percent of what doctors recommend that you eat each day. It's this fiber that helps move food through your digestive track more quickly while preventing constipation (because it makes you go to the bathroom more regularly). But stomach-smart as apples may be, if you find yourself suffering from any kind of digestive problem—like heartburn, constipation, bloating, or gas—check in with your doctor. She may prescribe a medication or help you trace the problem to a specific food intolerance. In many situations, simply cutting certain foods out of your diet may ease gastric problems.

CG! TIP: During the day, snack on brightly colored fruits and vegetables—like berries, carrot sticks, and apples—to add antioxidants to your diet.

butt seriously!

Q **"I have this really itchy feeling in my butt. I've wiped so hard sometimes that I see blood. Do you think this could be something extreme?"**

A This happens to almost everyone, and it's rarely serious. There are few causes: One is that even the smallest flake of stool left in the anal opening can irritate the skin, making it feel itchy. Another is what you're eating—spicy foods, citrus fruits, and caffeine can inflame the delicate tissue of the anus on their way out. Also, if you're taking antibiotics, the balance of bacteria in your intestinal tract may be thrown off, which can leave your anus susceptible to irritation. Other possible causes include hemorrhoids (swollen blood vessels in and around the anal opening) and skin tags (harmless hereditary bump-like growths). To get rid of the itch, keep the area clean and dry; wash in the shower without soap and use unscented toilet paper. Don't scratch the itch (even though it's tempting); apply cortisone cream for relief. Still itchy after a week? See your doctor for a prescription.

BODY BaSiCs

Q "I'm worried that I may have hemorrhoids. Is it really possible to get them at any age? How can I get rid of them?"

A Hemorrhoids are small (pea- to marble-size) lumps on the outside or inside of your anus. They might itch or burn, and you may be seeing bright red blood in your stool or on your toilet paper. Hemorrhoids are regular blood vessels that have become engorged with blood. Experts don't know why some people get them and others don't (um, luck?), but 50 percent of the population will experience them. Teens can get hemorrhoids, but many people who think they have hemorrhoids actually have a fissure (a small cut in the lining of the anus, which is often caused by pushing out a hard stool). Whether you have a fissure or a hemorrhoid, the same initial treatment applies: (1) Eat more fiber! Straining to push out a rock-solid stool will put more stress on that already tender skin. Eat whole grains, bran cereals, fruits, and vegetables. Also be sure to drink lots of water to avoid becoming dehydrated (or constipated) from all that fiber. (2) Taking Tylenol can help ease your pain. (3) Use Baby Wipes instead of toilet paper every time you have a bowel movement (t.p. can be abrasive) and be gentle—dab, don't scrub. (4) A warm bath and Preparation H will soothe irritated skin. Most hemorrhoids heal on their own in a few weeks, so if your pain doesn't go away after a month, talk to your doctor. (Don't be embarrassed! There's a 50 percent chance she's had them too!) She can discuss other options with you.

Q

"Since I was 10, I've had pimples on my behind. I wash, but they still show up. How can I: (a) prevent them; and (b) get rid of the marks?"

A

Even if you don't have a "hairy" butt, there are a lot of hair follicles there where bacteria can grow and cause mini-infections (a.k.a. pimples). Plus, clothing fits tightly over that area, making our butts even sweatier and more bacteria-prone. Try using a benzoyl peroxide wash like PanOxyl 5% soap bar in the shower to control outbreaks. Then wipe your cheeks with a salicylic acid acne pad morning and night. During exercise, wear breathable, loose-fitting cotton. If you have marks, it's just part of the healing process—but don't pick! Leave them alone; they should fade in three to six months. If they don't, see a dermatologist for treatment.

CG! TIP: When you feel a zit forming, take an anti-inflammatory, such as Advil. It will reduce the swelling that forms around the pimple.

crap you should know!

Q "Lately, it hurts me to poop—I get a sharp pain. There's no blood, but I still worry. Could it be because I'm overweight?"

A If you feel burning or stabbing sensations in your pelvis while you're pooping, it can be a sign of endometriosis. If that's the case, it has nothing to do with your weight; endometriosis is thought to be a hereditary condition. It occurs when the endometrium (the tissue lining in the uterus) starts growing outside the uterus. The reason it hurts when you go to the bathroom is that these endometrial implants live alongside the nerve pathways of the muscles you use during a bowel movement. The best thing to do is see your gynecologist for a checkup. And if you do have it (it affects 10 percent of teen girls), she can prescribe medication to prevent the implants from bleeding and growing.

CG! TIP: Looking for a great all-natural cure for constipation? Drink lots and lots of water!

Q "I don't like to go to the bathroom at school. I don't mind doing number-one, but number-two is much too embarrassing! Is it bad to hold it in?"

A It's fine to hold it in for a few hours. Even doing this regularly won't lead to any major problems—but it *can* cause discomfort like cramping, so it's best to just go when you have to. There's nothing to be embarrassed about—everyone does it! And this will probably make you feel a lot more confident: 55 percent of CosmoGIRL!s polled said they go when they have to go. That's more than half. So don't be scared! Relax and know that what you're doing is only natural!

CG! TIP: Sometimes reading helps you relax when you've gotta go, so always keep something to read in your bathroom!

BODY BASICS

Q "Why does my poop sometimes come out in pieces, not whole?"

A Poop comes in all shapes and sizes—sometimes it's long and thin, other times, it comes out in pieces, just as you have described. Don't worry—there's nothing wrong with you. But there are ways to avoid these small pieces. A high-fiber diet (wheats and grains, like brown rice and whole grain bread) makes stool more solid, which means it will hold together better. Also remember that the less you go, the more likely your stool will come out this way as the longer stool sits in your colon, the more likely it is to come out in little pieces.

CG! TIP: To get more fiber in your diet, eat complex carbs, like brown rice instead of white rice and whole wheat bread instead of white.

Q "Lately, I've been seeing traces of blood in my stool—is that bad? Do I have colon cancer? I'm only sixteen years old! Please help!"

A Don't worry, you probably don't have colon cancer. The most likely explanation is that just have a small tear in your anus. When the stool rubs against it, it causes it to bleed. But the blood *might* be a sign that you have an inflammation of the intestine, so see your doctor just in case.

Q **"I know poop is usually dark brown or black—mine usually is—but what does it mean if my poop is yellow or green?"**

A Poop starts off green, the color of bile (a fluid that aids in digestion to break down fat). But the hue changes depending on natural bacteria, what you eat, and how long it sits in your colon. If your poop is green, chances are, you haven't been holding on to it for that long.

CG! TIP: Always wipe front to back. Bacteria from the anus is bad for your vagina and could give you a UTI.

Q **"Not to be gross or anything, but I sometimes wonder if I poop enough. My mother and sister are like clockwork. Every morning before leaving the house, they go. I probably only go about every two days. I'm not constipated or uncomfortable or anything like that. I just don't go. Do you think I'm okay?"**

A Here's some good news: There is no such thing as a "normal" schedule. People generally go by their own schedules, and anywhere from twice a day to every other day is pretty much when people poop. As long as you're consistent, there shouldn't be a problem. If you find that you are starting to feel constipated and don't go for more than a few days at a time, you may want to try adding more fiber to your diet and drinking more liquids. This should keep things moving along just fine. If you're still having trouble after changing your diet, talk to your mom about seeing a doctor. It never hurts to make sure everything's working the way it should.

CG! TIP: Never force yourself to go. Straining or "pushing" may tear your anus, which can lead to more serious situations—like an infection.

weighty issues

Q "I'm really insecure about my weight. Actually, I've always been. For as long as I can remember, all my friends have been wearing at least a size— if not more—smaller than me, and when I hang out with them, especially when guys are around, I usually feel like the group blimp. If that's not bad enough, no boy I've ever liked has asked me out. What can I do to lose weight and get the guys I like to like me too?"

A It sounds to us like the most important thing going on here may not be your weight, but your self-esteem. If you're a size or two more than your friends who you see as "normal," chances are, you're not as large as you think you are. You're not alone in your insecurities. It seems like everyone's obsessed with body image. If you obsess over it, and talk about it all the time, chances are this is what's going on with you. But keep in mind: No guy wants to go out with a girl who repeatedly has to be told that her butt isn't too big. It's okay to want to take off a few pounds if your goal is a healthier body, but always be comfortable in your own skin. Lack of confidence is more of a turn-off than a few extra pounds. Before others can truly love you, you have to accept yourself for who you are.

CG! TIP: Never eat because you're feeling depressed, angry, or sad. That's the best way to put on pounds!

Q "I've been looking into dieting, but there are so many to choose from. Which one would you suggest?"

A With all the no-carb and no-fat diets out there, it can be tough to figure out what's *truly* good for you. But the key to eating healthy isn't cutting stuff out—it's eating just enough vitamin-rich foods, like veggies, lean meat, and multigrain breads, and cutting back on foods that have been processed, like frozen meals and packaged snacks.

CG! TIP: View the foods you eat as a way to get softer, shinier hair and stronger nails.

BODy BaSiCs

Q "I'm always on a diet, but I can't seem to lose any weight. I eat every good thing there is, but still, the pounds go on, not off. What can I do?"

A Sounds like you're eating healthily, but perhaps the reason you're not losing weight is because you're not controlling your portions. A 3-ounce piece of cooked chicken, fish, or lean meat is about the size of a cosmetic compact. One-half-cup-sized baked potato is about the size of a tennis ball. One ounce of cheese is about the size of a one-inch cosmetic wedge. One tablespoon of salad dressing is the size of a bottleful of nail polish. Compare these measurements with how you've actually been eating. Have you been overdoing it?

CG! TIP: Eat smaller portions. If you're still hungry twenty minutes after you eat, you can always add more to your plate.

Q "My mother and my friends tell me that I'm obese, but I tell them that I just like to eat. I'm only sixteen years old. I want to enjoy my life now, and I'll diet when I get to college and when I'm older. What's wrong with that?"

A We're sorry to say, but there are many things wrong with that. First of all, being overweight at any time in your life can be potentially dangerous. In addition to making you feel unattractive, there are many health risks associated with obesity. You can develop joint problems in your ankles and hips—and you could even risk dislocating your hips. Back pain is also common when you carry too much extra weight. And breathing, which should be as effortless as, well, breathing, also becomes a problem when you're obese. On top of that, you also risk shortness of breath and sleep apnea, which causes snoring and briefly stops you from breathing when you sleep—and can lead to serious heart disease later in life. And it only gets worse. Being excessively overweight, you can develop cysts on your ovaries, acne, male-pattern hair growth—like hair on our chin and chest—as well as irregular periods and even infertility. There's also a chance of developing diabetes, which brings with it a whole slew of problems, including fatigue, damage to your circulation, and eventually high blood pressure. In severe cases of diabetes, you can develop blindness, and if your circulation to your limbs gets so bad, you run the risk of hand and foot amputation. And don't forget about your liver! Fat accumulation in the liver can lead to liver damage and possible liver failure—and you may even need a transplant. So...Have we scared you skinny yet?

CG! TIP: Eat between meals—but healthy stuff. Fruit, veggies, and even hummus make great snacks every three to five hours.

Q "Until around 3:30 p.m., just look- ing at food makes me want to puke. So I usually skip breakfast and lunch. But then I get so hungry that I pig out. How can I stop?"

A Feeling sick at the sight of food is definitely not a good thing. But there might be a simple reason—and remedy—for it. Could it be that you just don't like the food you're faced with in the morning and at lunchtime? If breakfast means a greasy plate of fried eggs and bacon, and your stomach can't handle heavy food first thing, that can make you queasy. Like, even the sight of milk makes many people uneasy. The same goes for lunch: Cafeteria food isn't exactly known for winning Emeril's award for culinary excellence! But by not fueling your body for the most active parts of the day, you're forcing your brain to strain to concentrate. That causes your muscles to become sluggish and less responsive. Then when you finally do pig out, your body is forced to use the little energy it does have for diges- tion. That draws blood away from your brain and extremities, causing you to feel more sluggish and maybe a bit woozy. Instead of starving yourself, talk to your parents about fixing meals that include foods you'll look forward to eating. You might find that in the morning and early afternoon, you still need to eat lighter foods like breakfast bars, yogurt, pretzels, or a smoothie. And it's okay to eat several mini meals several times during the day. Bring portable snacks with you to eat when the mood strikes during school. By eating little meals throughout the day, you'll be much less likely to overeat after school.

But if none of this helps, you may have an eating disorder. If you still can't bear to put anything in your mouth before mid-afternoon, or, all day, you might have a problem called anorexia. If you are pigging out later in the day, you might have a problem called binge-eating disorder. Or, if you binge and then purge, you migh be bulimic. None of these are really about food—they're about having control. Anorexics, bulimics, and binge eaters use food (or lack of) to distract themselves from emotional problems, so to eat healthfully again, they need to deal with those issues with the help of a specialist trained in eating disorders. If these goes untreated, they can lead to complications including hair loss, high blood pressure, heart disease, and diabetes. So if you think you may have an eating disorder, check out the National Eating Disorder Association at **nationaleatingdisorders.org** or call 800-931-2237 for more information.

CG! TIP: Eat healthy snacks, like granola or fruit, two to three times a day to maintain your energy level. Low energy can make you feel stressed.

BODY BASICS

Q **"Are diet pills safe to use, and can you really lose weight from taking them?"**

A "Drop pounds painlessly!" "Burn fat while you sleep!" "Lose flab fast!" These diet-product pitches sound so enticing, but the fact is, they can be very dangerous. Here's why: Some diet pills on the market today have effects similar to those of the drug speed. They increases your heart rate and your metabolism, and burn more calories (that's how diet pills help you lose weight). Some diet pills have guarana (a substance that's like caffeine but much more powerful) to rev up your heart rate even more. And because some of these "natural" substances are considered dietary supplements rather than drugs, they aren't regulated by the Food and Drug Administration. That means that each pill can vary widely. Since you can't ever be sure how much you're taking, you could overdose without even realizing it. And worse, if you drink coffee or exercise while taking these pills, your heart rate could increase to the point where you over-stimulate your cardiovascular system. For some people, this may lead to cardiac arrest. So if you want to lose weight, check with your doctor. If she agrees that your health could be improved by dropping a few pounds, then the most effective method for losing weight and keeping it off is healthy eating and regular exercise. We know it sounds cliché, but it really is the only safe way. And don't shed more than a pound a week—max. Okay?

vegging out!

Q "Lately I've been thinking about becoming a vegetarian, but my mom's worried that I may be losing out on some important vitamins if I cut meat and fish out of my diet. How can I eat the way I want but still make my mom happy?"

A The first thing you should do before giving up meat is to consult a registered dietician. In fact, that's a good practice any time you're thinking of a drastic change in diet. Now you're probably going to hate hearing this, but your mom is absolutely right to be worried about you getting proper nutrition. You're still growing after all. If you really want to become a healthy herbivore, you need to make sure that you're getting certain vital nutrients that you used to rely on meat and fish for. One of the biggest ones you'll be missing is protein. Muscles, organs, antibodies (infection fighters) and hemoglobin (which oxygenates the body) are made of protein. To make sure you get this in your diet, eat lots of brown rice, beans, soy, eggs, dairy, and nuts. During your period, you lose lots of iron. If you don't replace it, you may become anemic, which will make you feel really tired. To get iron in your diet without eating meat, eat plenty of fortified grains and cereals, dark leafy greens, beans, and peas. Calcium, really crucial to building bone mass, is deposited into your bone bank through your early thirties. That means you want to get as much of this nutrient as possible now! Maximize calcium intake by eating lots of dark leafy greens, dairy, and calcium-fortified foods. (Check labels.) Zinc works hand-in-hand with iron; your body uses it to heal wounds and repair muscles and tissue. (It's also great for clearing your skin.) Vitamin B_{12} is good for red blood cells and your nervous system. Get this essential nutrient from fortified foods, eggs, and dairy products.

Here's another tip for a boost of nutrients: Use a cast-iron skillet when cooking so more iron will get into your food. Also, when you do make the change, be sure to drop meat gradually. Drop red meat first, then pork and poultry, then finally, fish.

CG! TIP: Looking for great ways to cook vegetarian? Visit **www.vrg.org** for lots of recipes and more information on the diet.

Q "What's the difference with types of vegetarians? I've heard that if I am a certain type of vegetarian, I can eat fish. Is that true?"

A Actually, there are four types of vegetarians—and *none* of them eat fish. Which of these you decide to become depends on why you're adapting the vegetarian diet. Lacto-ovo vegetarians eat only plant foods, plus eggs and dairy (milk, cheese, butter, and yogurt). Because it's the least restrictive off all the vegetarian diets, the only nutrient you'll have to worry about not getting enough of is iron. Lacto vegetarians eat only plant foods and dairy—no eggs. If you're on this diet, be sure to have at least two to three servings of protein a day, as well as iron. Ovo vegetarians eat only plant foods and eggs—no dairy, so the primary nutritional concerns with this eating style are iron, calcium, and vitamin D. Vegans eat strictly plant foods, so many essential nutrients are missing from this diet.

CG! TIP: Be sure to take supplements to get the necessary nutrients you may be lacking on a vegetarian or vegan diet.

ChApTeR 2

girl stuff

Lots of the things you read about in the last chapter
can happen to anyone. But stuff in this chapter? Well,
it's just for us girls! Do you worry about the same stuff
as other CosmoGIRL!s? Read on to find out.

getting abreast of things

Q "This may sound silly, but I think my breasts are too big. It's bad enough that I never fit into any of the cool clothes my friends wear, like babydoll T-shirts, but I'm also starting to have some pain in my back and neck. And let's not even get into how guys react to them. I was thinking about breast reduction surgery but I'm only seventeen years old. Is this a bad idea?"

A Reconstructive surgery is a choice every woman has to make for herself but only after thinking about the good and bad points and after talking it over with people you trust, like your mom. You should not rush into it, and being that you're under eighteen, chances are you won't be able to. Most doctors recommend waiting for your breasts to stop growing before performing the surgery. That said, there are definite plusses and minuses. For one, having a smaller chest will mean no more of that back pain that's been bothering you. And if you like sports, your big bust won't be bouncing in your way anymore. Just keep in mind what you're in for: surgery. Afterwards, you won't be able to move around much while your body tries to recover. Also, your scars won't fade for about six months so you won't want to sport a bikini anytime soon. And lifting your arms over your head or doing anything like that for a few weeks will be plenty painful. Do the pros outweigh the cons? Then go for it!

Q **"My breasts are pointy and triangular-shaped, not round like everyone else's. I'm 18, so I'm guessing I won't be growing out of this. Are there surgical procedures that can change the shape of your boobs?"**

A Just like you may inherit your mom's nose, like it or not, you may also inherit her breasts. Breast size and shape are hereditary, though gaining or losing weight can also make a difference. And breasts usually stop changing a year or two after your first period. So if you've already been menstruating for a few years, chances are your breasts are pretty much going to stay the way they are. But going under the knife to change what Mom gave you isn't necessarily the answer. We know you've heard this before, but cosmetic surgery can be dangerous, expensive—and may offer only temporary results. As you age, your "breast lift" may eventually start to sag. And breast implants can leak and cause various other health problems, including painful hardening of the breast tissue. Instead of hating your body, take a look around you the next time you're in a health club or a clothing store that has a communal dressing room. Seeing all of those women will make you realize that breasts come in all shapes and sizes. Yes, some are perfectly round and perky like the ones in Victoria's Secret ads, but more just aren't. The point is, non-round breasts are totally normal and natural—and they can be just as sexy and beautiful as any other types of breasts. Making peace with your proportions and learning to love and respect what you have up top makes you look—and feel—more comfortable in your own skin. And there's absolutely nothing sexier than that!

CG! TIP: Give yourself a quick breast exam in the shower or when you're lying in bed at night.

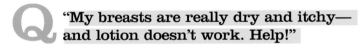

Q **"My breasts are really dry and itchy—and lotion doesn't work. Help!"**

A If your skin's dry *only* on your breasts, your bra may be too tight, causing chafing. Many girls don't know their correct bra size—go to a lingerie shop or department store and ask for a fitting. You could also be allergic to the fabric. If your boulder holder is made of, say, Lycra, try a cotton one. If you're *still* itchy, see a dermatologist. You may have eczema, which causes extremely dry skin—but can be treated.

Q "I have these red lines on my breasts, and I don't know how they got there. Are they normal? Will they go away?"

A Sounds like you've got stretch marks. A lot of us get them as teens because our breasts are growing faster than the skin around them, and the layers of tissue in the skin are stretched thin. Marks are red because deeper layers of skin are torn and swell. But within a year, they'll turn white as the inflammation goes away, and those will fade over time. You can have a dermatologist lighten your red stretch marks with a laser—but it costs $300 to $700 per session, and you'll need about three to five visits. Or, once they turn white you can use an Amino-Peptide complex treatment like Olay Regenerist Perfecting Cream that may help build skin. There's also a cream called Renova that might work even better. It's by prescription only, so ask your doctor about it. As a last resort, talk to your doctor about laser treatment and micro-abrasion. But lots of girls have stretch marks—so before you do anything drastic, try to accept that there's nothing weird about you!

CG! TIP: It's actually very common for one breast to be larger than the other—so don't worry—you're just like everyone else!

a bit nippy

Q **"I have something really weird to admit. My nipples stick in instead of out. It's kind of embarrassing. Why are they like this when it seems everyone else in the world's nipples stick out?"**

A Just as some people have "outie" belly buttons and others have "innies," up to 35 percent of girls have inverted or flat nipples. In other words, there are many other women and girls with nipples just like yours! And by the way, innies are just as sensitive as outies. You can breast-feed just as well, too, though it can be trickier for the baby to latch on. So when the time comes, ask your doctor how to make it easier.

Q **"My breasts aren't that big, but my nipples are huge! I don't think it's normal for people to have nipples this large. Why do I have this? Is it a problem? Is it hereditary?"**

A There's nothing to freak out about—you're completely normal. What you're probably talking about are not your actual nipples (the small part of your breast that sticks out when it's touched or exposed to the cold) but your areolas (which can range from light pink to dark brown). Their size is basically determined by one thing: genetics. In fact, you can bet someone in your family has areolas that look just like yours. (Have you asked your mom or grandmother about this? It might ease your mind.) And don't worry, your large areolas will *not* make you more likely to have a breast problem—or any other medical issue. So next time you're getting dressed in a locker room, just remember that the other girls are probably wondering if *theirs* are normal-sized too. And guess what? In most cases, they *are*.

CG! TIP: When it comes to breast and nipple size, there really is no such thing as "normal."

GiRl Stuff

Q "I 'nip out' every day. I nip through whatever I wear. Help!"

A Nipples (and the areolas around them) are the most sensitive parts of your breasts. When they get touched (in a sexual way or even just by shirt material) the tiny muscle cells under and around your nipples contract and look "hard." To hide them, wear a molded bra, which has a bit of padding (like Victoria's Secret T-shirt bra). Don't want any padding? Buy bras made of thicker, cotton-Lycra blends.

Q "What are those goosebump-y things on my nipples?"

A They're just the visible ends of the tiny oil glands that lie beneath your areola (the darkened patch of skin surrounding each nipple). Though you can see and feel them, these specialized oil glands aren't in use yet. Their purpose is to secrete a lubricating fluid so your nipples don't become dry and chafed when (and if) you breast feed. While these oil glands are often visible, they become noticeable if they get clogged (they'll also feel a little tender to the touch). Just leave the blocked gland alone (no popping!) and let it heal by itself. A warm washcloth will help ease any tenderness.

Q "My nipples leak twice a day. Is this normal?"

A Is there any blood? If so, see your doctor. Even though breast cancer is extremely rare in women under 25, it's better to get it checked out. No blood? It's most likely one of two things: (1) You're pregnant. Nipples often leak during pregnancy because breasts are producing milk for your baby. If you're sexually active, get a pregnancy test—pronto! (2) You or someone else is touching your nipples too much. When nipples are stimulated, your body can think it's from a baby; milk-producing hormones kick in, and sometimes milk can leak out. So try to keep your nipple stimulation to a minimum.

CG! TIP: Check your breasts for signs of cancer several days after your period ends, when they are least likely to be swollen and tender.

what's going on "down there"?

Q "I have a lump next to my vagina, near my leg. When I squeeze it, pus comes out. What is it?"

A Sounds like what you have is an infected hair follicle. It's not a big emergency—don't worry! You can usually get one of these by shaving—the razor can irritate your skin and let bacteria creep in. Even just wearing tight jeans can cause one by trapping sweat and germs in the follicle. But stop squeezing it! Instead, soak the area with a hot washcloth several times a day or try taking a few warm baths to bring the swelling down and help it heal.

Q **"My crotch is fat. It shows through my bathing suits and tighter clothes. Is there anything I can do?"**

A The vulva (the external part of your genitals) has a significant amount of fat beneath the skin and vulvas vary in size as a result. Having a large one is normal, and there's nothing you can do to change its size. But since this happens only with tight-fitting clothes, try wearing pants and bathing suits that have a little more material in the front panel. That way, your vulva won't show through and your clothes will hug your curves exactly the way you want.

CG! TIP: Vaginas come in many different shapes and sizes—there really is no such thing as a "normal" size or shape when it comes to yours!

Q **"I'm confused...I scrub my vagina clean, but have a whitish discharge and odor. Also, I douche often, but for some reason, I occasionally have a strong, fishy odor and creamy beige discharge coming from there. What's going on?"**

A It may sound strange, but that whitish discharge acts as a natural cleanser, sweeping harmful bacteria out of your vagina. And the daily odor is the scent of the discharge mingling with your body's natural perspiration. Still, be sure to wash your vagina daily to prevent odor and bacteria from building up. While in the shower, lather up the entire area, front-to-back, and between your vaginal lips using a gentle unscented soap. (Don't scrub hard—the skin outside your vagina is delicate.) Then rinse. Douches or special cleansers should not be used. In fact, they may cause Bacterial Vaginosis (BV), which could explain the fishy odor and discolored discharge. This occurs when you have an overgrowth of certain vaginal bacteria. It's usually associated with sexual contact, but can also be caused by douching and wearing tight clothing. As BV could predispose you to more serious infections, such as pelvic inflammatory disease (PID), which can make you more susceptible to other STDs, be sure to see your doctor for a prescription.

Q **"I have been having a bubbly, greenish-yellow discharge from my vagina. There's also a bad stink. What's wrong with me?"**

A You might have trichomoniasis, or "trich," an STD caused by a vaginal parasite. You can get it from having sex with someone who has it, or, in very rare cases, by wiping improperly, which can contaminate your vagina. Other telltale signs: a rotten-garbage odor. Head to your doctor and get a prescription. If you don't treat trich right away, it can cause inflammation in your vagina and cervix, making you more susceptible to more serious STDs.

Q "Whenever I go to the bathroom, there is always a white sticky paste in my underwear. Is that normal?"

A No need to worry—that white discharge is totally normal. It's made up of harmless vaginal and cervical secretions that clean your vagina, flushing out bad bacteria so you don't develop an infection. The amount of discharge you'll see and just how often you'll see it depends on your hormone levels, which fluctuate throughout your menstrual cycle. Doctors estimate that about half of all women produce some kind of discharge, so if you're one of them, you may start seeing that "paste" a few months before you get your first period. Some girls (like you) will have discharge every day, but others will just notice it sporadically. In the days right before your period, discharge is usually thick, whitish to pale yellow in color, and somewhat sticky. Mid-cycle—about two weeks after your period ends—it may look a little different. At this point, it will likely be thinner and clearer with a mucous-like consistency. If it'll make you feel more comfortable, wear a thin panty liner to absorb the fluid. And always wear all-cotton underwear so air can circulate and leave you feeling drier. If your discharge is very different from usual, it's your body's way of signaling that you might have a health problem. Visit your gynecologist and see what's up. She may run some tests and tell you what's going on. You can also check the yellow pages under "clinics" or **ppfa.org** for the nearest Planned Parenthood. Most clinics are inexpensive, and you won't need your parents' consent.

Q "My vagina's been really itchy lately, and today, I had a white, chunky discharge. It also burns down there when I pee. Am I dying?"

A Sounds to us like what you have is a yeast infection. These can be triggered by antibiotics like tetracycline (used for acne) and ampicillin (for respiratory infections), as well as tight-fitting pants or non-cotton underwear. Other telltale signs are itching and burning. Even if you've had a yeast infection before and treated it with an over-the-counter remedy, it makes sense to see your doctor. You want to make sure that it's not another infection that you're confusing with a yeast infection.

Q "Is it possible to get an infection from my thong?"

A Thongs definitely prevent the dreaded panty-line, but they can also cause skin irritations, yeast infections, and urinary-tract infections. To protect yourself from these, choose natural fibers. Cotton or 50 percent cotton blends allow air to circulate to your vagina, preventing bacteria and yeast buildup. If your thong is too tight, the string of the thong will rub against the skin of your labia, helping bacteria and yeast to spread. So be sure to wear thongs that are not too tight. Go for more coverage where it counts. Wider panels of fabric covering your crotch are less irritating than skinny ones. Log on to **mastersonmd.com** to purchase panties in gyno-approved styles. When you're home, and panty lines don't matter that much, switch to bikini panties.

GiRl StuFf

Q **"I just got my second yeast infection. I'm worried—can this cause infertility?"**

A Yeast infections are common: 75 percent of women will get at least one in their lifetime. Symptoms include an itchy and sore vaginal area and an odorless, white, cottage cheese-y discharge. Here's the deal: Yeast (a.k.a. Candida albicans) is a fungus that exists naturally in your vagina. Wearing tight jeans or non-cotton undies, or hanging out in a moist bathing suit all day creates the perfect environment for yeast to grow out of control—and that's called a yeast infection. Other ways to bring on yeast include taking antibiotics (they can kill off the good bacteria that normally keep yeast in check), taking birth control pills, douching (it can alter the pH in your vagina), or even having a cold or flu. While yeast infections don't cause infertility, several other kinds of infections can. So you should be sure that what you have is really a yeast infection since some STDs (including gonorrhea and Chlamydia) and bacterial vaginosis (the most common type of vaginal infection) have very similar symptoms. And these infections can lead to infertility if they're not dealt with. If untreated, they can spread to your fallopian tubes and uterus, where they can cause scar tissue to build up. And that scar tissue can keep the egg and sperm from traveling and joining together properly, resulting in infertility. Bottom line: A yeast infection will not cause infertility. If you suspect you have a yeast infection, go to a doctor—because you need to know for sure. Studies show that nearly two-thirds of women who buy yeast-infection medicine don't actually have one! That's bad news, because if you try to treat an STD or vaginosis, you could mask its symptoms while the infection continues to grow, leading to the infertility problems we mentioned before. If your doctor sees that you do have a yeast infection, she'll prescribe a cream (such as Gyne-Lotrimin) or a single-dose pill (such as Diflucan), which will cure you in a week or less. And if you don't have a yeast infection, she'll determine what's wrong, and you'll get the treatment you need. Either way, your vagina will thank you.

CG! TIP: If you don't like wearing all-cotton undies, be sure to wear ones that at least have a cotton crotch. This will help you avoid getting a yeast infection.

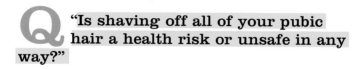

Q "Is shaving off all of your pubic hair a health risk or unsafe in any way?"

A Before you make a date with your razor, you should know that pubic hair is there for a few good health reasons. It provides a cushion that helps prevent your labia (the fleshy skin or "lips" around your vagina) from getting chafed, which can happen when you wear tight clothes or ride a bike. The hairs also act sort of like a spiderweb, trapping harmful bacteria so they can't get into your vagina and cause infections like vaginosis. Plus, urinary tract infections are often caused by bacteria from the anus—and if you have no pubes, there's a clear pathway for that bacteria to travel to your urethra (where you urinate from) and infect it. Shaving also poses a risk of ingrown hairs—when hairs curl back on themselves and get stuck under the skin, causing sore, painful pimples. And then there's the matter of using a sharp blade in a sensitive area that you can't see very well. If you knick yourself while shaving, the bacteria near your genitals could get into the cut and give you a skin rash. Why put yourself through the irritation, stinging, and redness? If you still want to shave, do this: (1) Soften hair with warm water; (2) Apply plenty of shaving cream; (3) Use a brand-new razor; (4) Shave gently in the direction that the pubic hair grows. Another option is waxing—which you should let a professional do. A salon can take it all off (a "Brazilian" wax) for $25 to $50. One final warning: Keep depilatories like Nair away from your genitals. The chemicals can burn your labia.

CG! TIP: Rub a thin layer of aloe vera on your bikini line after you shave or wax to keep skin soft and prevent ingrown hairs.

that time of the month

Q **"What is period blood anyway? Is there anything in it besides blood? What about those dark clumps?"**

A You get your period when your uterus sheds its lining (the thin veil that covers the uterine walls)—that's what the menstrual flow is. Besides blood, there's endometrial tissue and bacteria, plus mucus that blocks infection-causing bacteria from getting passed your cervix and into your uterus. The clumps you may see are harmless, congealed globs of blood, which form when you're lying down but flow once you get up.

Q **"My period is so heavy, I've ruined most of my pants! Could I bleed to death from getting my period?"**

A If you experience this heavy flow for a couple of hours on the first and second day of your menstrual cycle and then it tapers off, there's probably nothing wrong. But if you experience heavy bleeding around the clock (and have to change your tampons or pads every hour for at least one full day), or you find that you're bleeding more than seven days, you should check with your doctor, just to be safe. (It could be that you have a hormonal imbalance, which can be easily treated.)

GiRl STuff

Q **"How can I get rid of that smell I get whenever I have my period? Should I douche or use powders?"**

A The odor is perfectly normal. It occurs when bacteria in the blood on your pad or in your vagina is exposed to oxygen. Washing your genital area with mild soap and water is the best way to reduce odor. And since tampons block out a lot of oxygen, you'll lessen any smell by using them. But avoid douches, deodorant sprays, and powders—they can throw off the normal balance of bacteria in your vagina and cause infection.

Q **"I started using tampons a few months ago, but after I take out my tampon, my vagina hurts a lot. Why is this happening? Is it normal?"**

A If it hurts when you pull a tampon put, it means that you're using one that's too big for your body and/or oversized for your flow. Here's the deal: Any size tampon will usually slide in pretty easily because your vaginal opening is moistened with blood, making it more stretchy. But a too-large tampon will dry out your vagina, tightening up the skin inside and making the tampon stick. The solution? Try switching to "junior-sized" tampons. Unlike your current stash of regulars and supers, juniors are designed for a lighter flow. You might also want to try using a rounded-tip or "slender" (read: skinnier) applicator for your vaginal opening. If you're still not comfortable, remember that you don't have to use tampons at all. Nearly half the girls who responded to a recent CosmoGIRL.com poll said that they actually prefer pads.

CG! TIP: Afraid of Toxic Shock Syndrome? Use the lowest absorbency tampon you can, and wear a pad when you sleep.

Q "Do tampons cause cancer or Toxic Shock Syndrome (TSS)? I've read that they do."

A Research shows that tampons don't cause cancer—they're just as safe as pads. But they do pose a miniscule risk for TSS, which is caused when a tampon is left in for too long, spurring the Staphylococcus aureus bacteria in the vagina to grow rapidly and release toxins into the bloodstream. Symptoms include a fever and sunburn-like rash. TSS can also be fatal, but it's rare. To lower risk, change tampons every four to six hours.

GiRl StuFF

Q "I'm fourteen years old and I'm worried that my period isn't regular. Just about all my friends get theirs every twenty-eight days or so, and it seems like mine comes every three to six weeks. Is there something wrong with me?"

A Don't worry. It's normal for your period to be irregular, especially when you are only fourteen years old. For about the first two years that you get your period, it can be hard to predict when you'll get it—it may come twice in one month or only once every three months. Your body is fine-tuning its cycle. Doctors don't know exactly why cycles can be irregular at first, but after a few years, it should settle into a cycle that runs between 28 and 35 days. If it doesn't, see your gynecologist.

Q "I'm fifteen years old and I'm embarrassed to say that I haven't gotten my period yet. I feel like I'll never get it! Help!"

A The age range for first-timers is about 10 to 16 years old. If you're on the older end of the first-time spectrum, you could just be a late bloomer. If you want to put your mind at rest, however, your best bet is to see a gynecologist just to be sure. She can help you rule out anything else that might be holding nature up!

Q **"For the past few months, just before I get my period, I feel like I want to scream and cry all the time, and I have no patience for anything—or anyone. I also feel really bloated and tired. What's wrong with me?"**

A Sounds like it may be PMS. Premenstrual Syndrome (PMS), which can happen the week before you bleed, still isn't completely understood by doctors—but they believe fluctuating hormone levels trigger uncomfortable symptoms like breast tenderness and bloating. There are over-the-counter remedies to treat PMS, and many also believe that foods, like chocolate, which releases serotonin, a chemical that makes you happy, and herbal tea, a diuretic, which helps alleviate bloating caused by water retention, are also very helpful remedies. Everyone's different: Check with your doctor to see if there's anything she can recommend.

CG! TIP: Drink water to lessen bloating (you'll pee more, releasing water) and to keep your skin clear.

GiRl StuFF

Q "I'm really scared what this could mean, but sometimes I bleed between periods. Is it possible that I have cervical cancer or something like that?"

A Are you on the Pill? If you are, we have a pretty easy answer for you. Light spotting (a.k.a. breakthrough bleeding) is common during your first three months on the Pill, and can also happen when you aren't taking your pill at the same time every day. If you're not on the Pill, it's not likely that you have cancer, but to put your mind at ease, why not make an appointment with your gynecologist?

CG! TIP: Period pain? Turn up the heat to relax muscles and soothe pain. Warm baths or disposable heat wraps work well.

Q "**Every time I get my period, I also get these horrible cramps. Some months they hurt so bad, I can't even get out of bed. Sometimes I even feel like I want to throw up! What causes them—and how can I make them stop?**"

A Cramps during your period are very common. They're caused by the uterus contracting to shed its lining. Those contractions may cause diarrhea and nausea. For pain relief, try these tips: Exercise speeds your blood flow and helps wash cramp-inducing chemicals out of your system. It also releases endorphins in your body, which reduces pain. Drink water to lessen bloating and to keep your skin clear. Turn up the heat to relax muscles and soothe pain. Warm baths or disposable heat wraps work well. Also, take 200 milligrams ibuprofen (like in Advil or Motrin) every four to six hours to relieve cramps. Herbal tea is also known to be helpful. For a really effective herbal tea, steep raspberry leaves with a decaffeinated tea bag (caffeine will cramp you up even more!) in boiling water and drink up! The heat of the tea relaxes the uterus and can prevent those contractions. Raspberry leaves have been used for years to alleviate cramps, though doctors are not sure why this plant is so soothing.

CG! TIP: Got cramps? Exercise speeds your blood flow and helps wash cramp-inducing chemicals out of your system, and it releases endorphins (which reduce pain) into your body.

Chapter 3

healthy body and healthy mind

Feeling stressed? Overwhelmed? Depressed? You're not alone! Read on about all the kinds of issues other CosmoGIRL!s are dealing with.

down in the dumps

Q **"For a while now, there are stretches of time when I feel really bummed for no reason. Nothing bad happens, but I still feel down. It doesn't last for long, maybe a few days. Still, I'm afraid it might get worse and maybe I'll become suicidal. What should I do?"**

A Sounds like you've got the blues. It's normal to feel gloomy once in a while—hormonal changes in your body (before or during your period) and the daily stress of school and relationships can sometimes put you in a funk. These blahs should pass soon. Combat your mood by doing something energizing. Running or dancing will trigger your brain to release those feel-good endorphins.

Q **"I'm really tired and sad lately—life isn't much fun, but I manage to get by I guess. I've felt like this almost every day for the past few months. Do you think I should see a therapist?"**

A You could be suffering from dysthymia (pronounced dis-THIGH-mee-a), a low-level depression. It's when you can take care of everything you need to get done, but you have to put a lot more effort into it—and you never feel satisfied with what you accomplish. If you don't take care of it, this could turn into major depression. Ask a parent or teacher about counseling.

CG! TIP: Losing 90 minutes of sleep will reduce your daytime alertness by 32 percent. So think twice about staying up for Conan!

Q "I feel so empty and I have no energy lately. I don't want to see anyone or do anything anymore. For more than two weeks, I've been thinking that the world might be better off without me. How can I stop feeling this way?"

A You may have a major depressive disorder known as clinical depression. Common symptoms of this are losing interest in things you used to love to do, feeling a deep sense of sadness, and thinking about suicide. You *can* feel better—if you get help. And you owe it to yourself to do just that. To find a professional to talk to, call the Depression and Bipolar Support Alliance at 800-826-3632.

HeAlThy BoDy & MiNd

Q "I haven't been feeling myself lately. My mother took me to the doctor, and she said that I was probably experiencing a 'chemical imbalance.' What exactly does this mean and how will medication help me?"

A Everyone has chemicals in their brain—like epinephrine, dopamine, and serotonin—that influence moods, emotions, and behavior. But experts believe that some people's brains burn through these chemicals too rapidly—like a gas-guzzling car—so they end up feeling irritable and depressed. Antidepressants correct and regulate chemicals in your brain so that they stay regulated even after you go off them. Selective serotonin reuptake inhibitors (SSRIs) are one type of antidepressant. SSRIs are not an instant cure—you can't just pop one to get a lift on the spot. It takes four to six weeks for some to work, since the medicine needs to build up in your bloodstream and in your brain before it can have an effect. And antidepressants don't work if you're not depressed (just like aspirin only lowers your body temperature if you actually have a fever). Once your symptoms have subsided, you usually need to stay on the medication for another 6 to 12 months—then you should consult your doctor about weaning yourself off.

CG! TIP: Stress headache? Pinch the tops of your toes using your thumb and index finger and squeeze for ten seconds, then release. Repeat two to three times until your headache is history.

Q "I've heard antidepressants can lead to suicide. I'm scared because I just got a prescription to take them. Am I going to be okay?"

A Antidepressants as a whole have helped many people, in fact, 10 percent of CosmoGIRLS! have taken anti-depressants. But SSRI's became controversial in 2003, when the British government warned health providers against giving teens any SSRI other than Prozac. That warning said that these drugs' effectiveness in young people hasn't been proved—and that they are linked to suicidal thoughts and self-harm in people aged 18 and under. Currently, the U.S. Federal Drug Administration (FDA) asks manufacturers of all antidepressant drugs to include warning labels and expanded warning statements that alert health care providers to an increased risk of suicidal thinking and behavior in [teens] being treated with these drugs. For updates on the FDA's review, go to **fda.org** and enter "antidepressants" into the search field. But the point isn't to be scared of these drugs; just educate yourself about them so you can take precautions. If you think you might be depressed, talk with your doctor about your options—talk therapy, anti-depressants, or a combination of both. Together you and your doctor can decide what is best—and safest—for you.

Q "I think I need therapy, but I heard it's really expensive. My mother just lost her job, and I don't want to be a burden on my parents right now. But I could really use some help figuring stuff out. Is there such a thing as 'cheap' therapy? Also, does going into therapy mean that I'm nuts?"

A Actually, there is. But let's look at all the options. Therapy might not be as expensive as you think. In fact, it may not cost you anything at all. Your parents' insurance may cover your therapy sessions, and many schools have staff psychologists and guidance counselors who are trained to deal with your emotional needs and do it for free. They can direct you to other professionals, like social workers, if you need more help. There are also low-cost or free therapeutic services at churches, clinics, and hospitals, as well as programs that over services on a sliding scale (meaning you pay only what you can afford). To find one near you, call the National Mental Health Organization at 800-969-6642 and say "I'm interested in low-cost therapists or counselors in my area—can you refer me to one?" Taking the step to get help means that you realize you're really sane. You can see clearly right now that you're not doing as well as you could be—and you want to do something about it. Therapy gives you the chance to examine things in your life with someone who can be more objective than family and friends can. It also helps you learn effective ways to problem-solve and gives you coping tools you can use throughout your life. And, we're right there with you: 27 percent of CosmoGIRL!s have seen a therapist.

Q "I'd like to try going to therapy, but I don't want to be committed to going for life. Is it possible to just do therapy for a little while and then stop when I'm feeling better?"

A How long therapy lasts depends on the seriousness of your problem and how quickly you are able to resolve it. Therapies for specific incidents—like a rape, or the death of someone close to you help you deal with that one thing. Once you're feeling better, you and your therapist can agree to be done. Other types of therapy, like those where the root of your problems is suspected to lie in a childhood trauma, can take longer. Talk to a counselor about what you want to deal with and the type of treatment that's right for you.

CG! TIP: Meditation is a great way to relieve stress in your life.

Q "Lately I haven't been feeling very good and I wish I felt better. It's not a physical thing—my body's working fine. It's emotionally that's the problem. I'm a wreck! How can I make myself feel better?"

A A healthy mind is just as important as a healthy body. So why not treat them both with the same kind of thoughtful care? Think about it: You use your mind to tap into valuable life tools like willpower, focus, and drive. And if you're not able to muster the determination to go after your goals or the optimism to bounce back from an awful defeat, you can't lead the life you deserve. Now we're not pushing antidepressants or therapy, but just know that you do have those options if venting to a friend, journaling, and exercising don't seem to cut it. Check in with yourself on a regular basis. It's essential for your happiness!

CG! TIP: Indulge yourself with chocolate! Studies have shown that it releases serotonin, a feel-good natural chemical, into your system.

Q **"Sometimes I get so focused on what I'm doing, I lose track of everything else going on in my life. I've heard this is a symptom of OCD. Could I have that?"**

A OCD usually involves obsessions and compulsions, but a person may only have one. Obsessions are thoughts, images, and impulses that occur over and over and feel out of your control. Compulsions are acts you perform to make your obsessions go away (like, if you're obsessing with germs, you might constantly wash your hands). For more information about OCD and treatment for it, visit **ocfoundation.org**.

CG! TIP: Listening to Mozart for 10 minutes while studying could boost your brain power by helping you become more focused.

the abcs of Zs

Q **"I have a hard time sleeping at night. I'm in a half-asleep, half-awake state until it gets light outside, and then I finally fall into a deeper sleep. I've been getting sick and losing weight lately. Could my lack of rest be the reason?"**

A Sleep is vital for keeping your immune system strong. If you're not getting the proper rest, you can become more susceptible to illnesses. Being sick could affect your appetite, and eating less makes you lose weight. But any time you are losing weight and aren't sure why, you should visit your doctor. She'll want to rule out problems like mononucleosis, chronic fatigue syndrome, and hyperthyroidism. Assuming you're healthy, other things could be sabotaging your sleep. Sometimes unresolved issues can cloud your mind as you're trying to fall asleep. Take some time during the day to identify the reasons you're overwhelmed, and then focus on just one thing at a time. A journal can help you release your feelings. Also try exercising earlier in the day—it's a great stress reliever. Still can't sleep? Use these tips to get your Zs: Stay away from caffeinated beverages or daytime cold medicine after 3 p.m.— they can make you too wired to nod off. And avoid watching television, taking phone calls, playing video games, or exercising at least an hour before bed, since they can overstimulate your body and mind and keep you awake. Finally, create a routine of five or so things to do each night before hitting the sheets.

Q "I have a horrible time sleeping at night. I wake up once or more every night, and I always feel cranky, irritable, and tired throughout the day. You would think this would mean that I'd be tired at night, but no. It usually takes me hours to fall asleep. How can I break this cycle?"

A You're right on target by calling your sleep situation a "cycle" that you need to break. Good news: You can! Try and go to bed every night so that your body will be on a regular schedule and know when it's time to start "shutting down." Exercise daily. Just 20 to 30 minutes of exercise a day will help you release the stress and energy that can keep you up at night. Don't eat late. Avoid heavy meals and snacks at least an hour before bed, your body will still be digesting, making it hard for you to sleep. Keep your room dark, quiet, and cool (68 degrees is ideal)—womblike conditions help you fall into a deeper sleep. Open your shades at least slightly to let the sun stream in in the morning. Do the same activity every night before going to bed. You're body will come to see this ritual as a signal to sleep and relaxation. Finally, get your fix of java (or other stimulants like sugar) before 2 p.m. to avoid being wired and wide awake later on. Within a few days, you should be back to normal again.

CG! TIP: Try not to nap after 4 p.m. or for longer than 35 minutes, or you may have trouble falling asleep.

Q "I snore all night and I feel like I never get any sleep as a result. I'm tired all the time during the day, and sometimes I even have a sore throat. Is there anything you can recommend to help me stop snoring?"

A Many people think that snoring at night is just an inconvenience when it actually could lead to more problems, like sleep apnea, and therefore should be treated. One thing you can try is to elevate your neck and head on two pillows. Also, try sleeping on your side. This will help open your airway. If you're still not having any luck, try an anti-snore spray like SilentSnore. And if all of these fail, be sure to see your doctor. When there's not enough room for air to pass through your throat, sleep apnea (often caused by obesity in teens), causes brief interruptions in your breathing while you sleep.

CG! TIP: Looking for a quick pick-me-up? Forget about coffee and soda. Energy-boosting water is a more effective and healthier choice.

Q "Last week I had finals, and to study, I pulled lots of all-nighters. Now I can't for the life of me get back on a normal sleep schedule. I stay up too late and I oversleep every day. It's driving me nuts! Do you have any suggestions?"

A It seems really annoying now, but if you discipline yourself, it will actually be really easy to get back on track with your sleeping habits. Here's what you should do: (1) Wake up tomorrow morning no later than an hour after your normal time. (2) Nap midday for 35 minutes. (3) Go to bed at your normal time. (4) Wake no later than half an hour later than normal time. If this doesn't work, examine your habits. Are you drinking caffeine too late? Are you under a lot of stress? Both of these have been known to throw off sleep schedules, so pay attention to them.

CG! TIP: Sleep loss is cumulative, so if you can't get all the sleep you need during the week, catch up on weekends.

Q **"No matter what I do, I always seem to wake up during the night, and I can't get back to sleep. What should I do?"**

A It's frustrating to be woken out of a sound sleep, only to struggle with getting back to those blissful Zs. But trying to force sleep makes it harder to relax, so don't force yourself to go back to sleep. Instead, do a quiet activity like reading for 20 minutes. Once you're calm and relaxed from reading, try to sleep again. If you're still up after 20 minutes, get up and start your day—the next night you'll be tired and more likely to sleep well.

Q **"I'm in my junior year in high school and I feel like I'm going to snap at any minute. I cry all the time, and I can't focus on the things I need to get done to get into a good college. Help!"**

A Sounds like you're under a lot of stress, but try not to feel hopeless. Stress is about how in-control you feel. Put your stresses into two lists: things I can change (college stress) and things I can't (your parents' divorce). Take charge of the "I can't" list by talking to a counselor (even asking for help puts you in control). And for the "can" list, make a de-stressing plan. Map out a college application schedule into manageable chunks (college visits, essay due dates). Once you have all you have to worry about organized into these small, neat, little piles, you'll be better equipped to dealing with them and you won't be running around driving yourself—and everyone around you—nuts!

ChAPTeR 4

the big "S"

When it comes to sex, everyone has questions. Heck, even experts don't know everything! We're willing to share everything we know, so get answers to some of your most private questions—without having to ask!

ThE BiG "S"

the right time?

Q **"All of my friends lost their virginity at a young age. What is a healthy age for me to start having sex?"**

A A "healthy age" means being smart about your health and emotionally mature—it's more about listening to your inner voice. Ask yourself: Do I want to have sex just to get it over with? Is it uncomfortable for me and my boyfriend to talk about birth control? Lots of girls lose their virginity just to "do it," and they're disappointed with what sex turns out to be. Or, since birth control isn't discussed beforehand, they put themselves at risk for pregnancy and STDs. You don't want that, so if you answered yes to either question, wait. A healthy age is when you're sure you'll have no regrets.

Q **"When will I know it's time to have sex with my boyfriend? We've fooled around a lot, and it's starting to become inevitable. But I just don't feel ready yet."**

A Just because you've fooled around with a guy doesn't mean you have to have sex (or do anything physical you're not comfortable with). If you do it just because he wants to, you'll only feel used. (Plus, you could get a bad rep, which would suck.) There's nothing that says you can't take the lead, so step up for what you want (or don't want) with him. Chances are, he'll find your confidence and honesty truly sexy—and he'll like you not just for your body but for who you are.

Q "I hear some girls need to get 'stretched' in order to have sex or it will be painful. I'm a virgin, and that scares me. How do I know if I need to get stretched?"

A You most likely have nothing to worry about. Some girls are born with Mayer-Rokitansky syndrome, a condition in which the vaginal canal is smaller than normal and has to be "stretched" to an average size. But it's extremely rare (only 1 in 5,000 girls in the U.S. has this condition). The doctor stretches the vagina by inserting a thin, plastic tube called a dilator into the vaginal canal. Most girls do experience soreness the first time they have sex because their vaginal walls expand from the pressure of the penis. But that pain is natural. If you're scared to have sex, it might be because you're not emotionally ready or you haven't found the right guy yet. So consider these things before you have sex for the first time.

ThE BiG "S"

Q **"Something's been bothering me. My boyfriend and I only hook up when we're wasted. Is this normal?"**

A Maybe the reason you're getting wasted before you fool around is because you don't feel comfortable about what you're doing. Alcohol and drugs numb the inner voice that may be telling you that you're not ready to have sex. Instead of trying to drown that voice out, listen to it. Deep down, you'll know when sex is right for you. And when you are ready, you'll want to be in control and remember it.

> **CG! TIP:** Think before you drink. Teenagers who drink alcohol are seven times more likely to have sex than teens who stay sober.

Q **"My boyfriend and I have never really talked about having sex before, but we've been together nearly six months and I feel like it's time we did. But how do I approach this with him?"**

A You don't want sex to be something that "just happens." Even though it looks spontaneous in the movies, you should be able to talk about it with your partner beforehand, so that it happens when you're prepared, with someone who loves you, at a time (and place) when you feel secure. A study by the National Campaign to Prevent Teen Pregnancy found that 72 percent of girls who had sex wish they'd waited. We're not saying you'll definitely regret it, but if the topic of sex hasn't come up, it might be because one (or both) of you just isn't comfortable doing it.

Q "My boyfriend and I have been talking about having sex, but I've been reluctant to go to the gyno to get birth control pills. He says he'll take care of the birth control, but why do I not feel one hundred percent like this is the right thing to do?"

A You may not be ready to have sex if you're not ready or willing to take responsibility for birth control. Listen, if you get pregnant, you're the one who's going to suffer the greatest consequences. He has the option to bolt; you don't. The simple fact is that not taking care of yourself isn't smart—or mature—so if you don't want to deal with the birth control part, you definitely aren't psychologically ready to get into the sex part. Not to be rude, but that's the truth.

CG! TIP: If you can't talk to your boyfriend about having sex, chances are you're not ready to have it.

ThE BiG "S"

Q **"I've been having sex for a few months now and I feel like I've been lying to my parents because I've been hiding it from them. Should I get over my guilt or should tell my parents? And if I do tell them, what's a good way?"**

A It's easier said than done getting over guilt. Clearly, you don't feel comfortable sneaking around with the sex thing and you want to tell them more than you don't want to tell them. This means you probably should. But a little advice: Do it when they're in a good mood (if they're already stressed, it may hard for them to take this news in stride). Say, "Mom and Dad? There's something important I want to tell you." That will prepare them. Keep in mind that the TV news has already told them that teens are having sex, so even if they're hoping you aren't, they know you could be. Then say, "Most kids would never tell their parents this, but I wanted to be honest with you. Kevin and I have started to have sex." Okay, so at first they might be shocked and think, My kid's having sex—I've failed! So you need to reassure them that you're in love, the relationship is monogamous, and you're practicing safe sex. By answering these questions about your emotional and physical health before your parents even ask them, you're helping them see that you're taking care of yourself, which is one of their main worries (because they love you and do worry!). Of course, they probably won't love the idea that you're having sex, but if you prove to them that you're in control of your decision, it'll be much easier for them to accept it. Good luck!

making sense of sex

Q **"Is sex as fulfilling and enjoyable as it looks on TV and in the movies?"**

A Sex can definitely be fulfilling and enjoyable, but it doesn't always resemble what you see on-screen. The media shows a fantasy version of sex rather than the sometimes confusing, uncomfortable, and/or messy reality. Think about it: When you turn on the tube, you always see two perfect-looking people magically melding together—no mention of insecurities, much less sexually transmitted diseases or pregnancy. Both partners always know what to do, and no one is nervous or discusses whether or not they're emotionally ready. So, just as the media romanticizes high-school life, dating, and friendships, it also shows sex in a too-perfect light. That's not to say sex isn't exciting and wonderful; it can be. But in real life, it's much more fulfilling when both partners feel at ease with themselves and are mature enough to discuss some very unsexy issues first—stuff you rarely see on-screen.

ThE BiG "S"

Q "Whenever I see something sexy on television or hear something sexy on the radio, I get turned on. What's going on?"

A Don't worry! It's completely normal to find yourself turned on by sexy sights and sounds like reading a racy novel, watching a very steamy video or a movie, or even listening to a sexy song. As your sexual organs mature and your hormones kick in, those sexy sights, sounds, tastes, and smells trigger the kind of brain chemicals that cause physical changes such as flushed skin, vaginal lubrication, a racing heart, or goosebumps (or all of the above). Plus, watching a sexy movie or listening to a sexy song may trigger a memory of a past sexual experience or fantasy. That, in turn, stimulates a physical reaction—those same body sensations we just talked about.

> **CG! TIP:** Don't be concerned if you find certain songs or movies sexy and your friends don't. Everyone is different!

Q **"I've had sex but felt no pleasure. It doesn't even feel good when I put my fingers inside myself. Am I weird?"**

A You're not weird at all. You might just be numb to sexual feelings right now because you're feeling guilty or just plain uncomfortable about having sex or touching yourself sexually. You need to take a step back and realize that there's nothing wrong with your body—really! You're just learning how your body works, and sex or sensual touching takes practice and, most important, mental readiness for it to feel good. It definitely sounds like you had sex before you were ready. So why not wait for the time to be right?

Q **"Looking through a book of phobias, I found one that fits me: erotophobia— a fear of having sex. Am I totally weird?"**

A We doubt there's anything "wrong" with you. It's normal for teens to feel anxious about (or even be afraid of) having sex. In fact, it would be unusual if you *weren't* nervous about taking this major life step! Besides the scary consequences of STDs and unintended pregnancy, sex involves some heavy emotions you may not be ready to deal with yet. Our advice: Don't second-guess your anxiety— listen to what your body is telling you it isn't ready to do. But if you *still* think you're worrying than most girls your age, go to the National Institute of Mental Health Web site at **nimh.nih.gov**. They can tell you where to get help for anxiety disorders such as erotophobia.

ThE BiG "S"

Q "I know when you have sex for the first time you bleed, but how much?"

A Actually, not everyone bleeds the first time she has sex. The hymen is a thin membrane that partially blocks the opening of your vagina. During first-time intercourse, it usually tears and can bleed—about the same amount you'd see from a small cut on your finger. But using tampons or even riding a bike can tear the hymen before you lose your virginity. If that's the case, you probably won't bleed during first-time sex because there's no hymen to break.

CG! TIP: You control your body, and you should always go at your own pace—even if you're not a virgin anymore.

Q "I've never had an orgasm. Is something wrong with me?"

A Absolutely not. Lots of women don't experience orgasm until they're in their twenties—after they have had more experience with guys and feel more comfortable with their bodies. Orgasm occurs when arousal builds and causes the muscles in your genital region to tighten and release in a wave of pleasure. Research shows that 24 percent of women have trouble reaching orgasm either alone or with a partner, so you're not the only one! And keep in mind that you're young, so you have plenty of time to experience it.

Q "This is kind of embarrassing to admit, but I masturbate a lot—like several times a week. I've heard different things about masturbation being both good and bad. Is it really normal to masturbate?"

A Your hormones kick in between the ages of 9 and 17. That prompts a lot of sexual energy. Masturbation (stimulating yourself sexually) is one way that some people release that energy. Strange that something believed to be so common is rarely talked about, huh? But the M-word makes some people feel shameful or guilty, maybe because they've been taught that touching their body in a pleasurable way is "dirty." Others think that only "desperate" people (meaning those not having sex) masturbate. But lots of sexually active people do it. The bottom line is that masturbation is a private thing that you shouldn't feel ashamed of doing or not doing. It can be a problem if you feel that you masturbate too often (like, you do it instead of doing things you used to enjoy). Go to **teenwire.com** to learn more.

ThE BiG "S"

Q **"I want to buy a vibrator, but I'm scared that if I do, my parents or sister might find it. Help!"**

A We'd love to say "don't let fear of your family's reaction stand in the way." But it *would* be pretty embarrassing if they found it. Since it's mature of you to want a vibrator, you could give them a mature explanation: "I didn't want to depend on a guy for sex, and I figured this way was safer." But if you'd rather die than say that, and because there's no guarantee they *won't* find it, you might just want to wait until you're in college or out of the house before you make this purchase.

> **CG! TIP:** No matter what you may have heard, no one has ever gone blind from masturbating.

Q **"I've heard of this thing called the G spot. What it is"**

A The G spot, which is named after Ernst Grafenberg, the gynecologist who discovered it, is a spongy, walnut-sized area of tissue located about three inches inside the vagina, along the front wall and toward your belly button. Known as the "second pleasure button" (the clitoris is the first), the G spot is an orgasm trigger. All women have a G spot, but since it can be hard to locate and stimulate during sex, many women don't have orgasms from it.

Q "I read an article about this girl who had a 'desensitized clitoris'—it said she had no feeling in that area. I'd really like to know more about it."

A Prolonged horseback riding or cycling (the kind a professional who's training for a long race does) can cause desensitization of the clitoris because of the constant pounding on that area. When the nerves of the clitoris are overstimulated, they retract and become numb in order to protect themselves. Wearing padded shorts can help prevent this from happening. Also, using a high-frequency, battery-operated vibrator too much can desensitize the clitoris. Just so you know!

Q "I want to have sex, but I have my period. Is there anything I can do to make it end sooner?"

A You can't stop your period once it's started, but you can predict when you get it by taking birth control pills. The Pill regulates your cycle so you get your period every 28 days, like clockwork. It can also make your flow lighter and make your period last for fewer days. And remember, if you and your boyfriend truly respect each other, then not having sex a few days a month shouldn't be a big deal.

ThE BiG "S"

take control of birth control

Q **"Lately I've been thinking about going on the Pill. I've heard there are benefits to it, even if you're not having sex. Can you tell me some of the other ways the Pill might be good for me?"**

A It's true, the main job of the pill is to prevent pregnancy; however, there are other pluses—and minuses—involved. On the plus side, certain Pill prescriptions are specially designed to clear up acne. Also, it can ease menstrual cramps and make your periods lighter and more regular. It can even help keep PMS under control. On the down side, the Pill can cause you to experience unpleasant side effects, like nausea and headaches. Some Pill prescriptions have also been known to cause vaginal dryness and a lessened libido. But there are many different Pills available; if you're having a hard time with one prescription, your doctor can always find another one better suited to your body chemistry. So speak up!

Q **"I'm on the Pill, and I find the first couple of days or so in each cycle, it makes me really sick. I get headaches and I feel nauseated. What happens if I throw up a pill?"**

A Essentially, if you don't take all your pills, you run the risk of getting pregnant. If you've thrown up your birth control pill, then take the next pill in your pack right away. This will cause you to get your period a day early, but it will at least cover you for the days you're taking it. But be careful—it won't be as effective as usual. Just to be safe, use a condom for the rest of your cycle (as you should anyway, to avoid STDs).

Q **"I have bronchitis and my doctor gave me a prescription for an antibiotic. I've heard these can affect the way the Pill works. Is this true?"**

A Most antibiotics don't interfere with the Pill. But to check on a particular prescription, call the toll-free help line on your pill packet or the pharmacy where you got the Pill just to be sure.

CG! TIP: There are many varieties of birth control pills out there. If one type doesn't agree with you, talk to your gynecologist about trying another.

ThE BiG "S"

Q "I was sleeping over my friend's house last week and I forgot my pills. She gave me one of hers. Will I be okay?"

A Be careful! Don't think you can just "borrow" pills from friends if you forget yours. This could be very dangerous for you and your friend. If she has a different prescription than you, you may get the wrong dose of hormones, which could cause spotting. Not to mention that she'll be a pill short! The best advice we can give you: If you forget your pills, go home and get them!

Q "I've heard that if I take my Pill at different times during the day, that I might get pregnant. Is this true?"

A The Pill is most effective if you take it at the same time daily to keep hormone levels steady. But as long as you do it within a three-hour window every day, you should be fine.

Q "I saw an ad for the birth control patch on TV, and I was wondering...is it as effective as the Pill?"

A The patch and the Pill put hormones in your blood to stop ovulation and prevent pregnancy. They are both safe and more than 95 percent effective, and they also cost about the same. Here's the difference: With the pill, you have to remember to take it every day at the same time. With the patch, you slap it on once a week. (Don't worry: The patch is sweat-proof, so it won't fall off. And it won't hurt to remove it like a Band-Aid does, because you wear it on smooth, relatively hair-free spots like your butt cheeks or back.) Be warned: If you get headaches or nausea from the Pill, you may have the same problems with the patch. And like the Pill, the patch is no shield against diseases like HIV and syphilis. You'll need to use a condom along with the Pill or the patch to protect yourself from STDs.

CG! TIP: Because the Pill is most effective when you take it at the same time every day, work taking the Pill into your routine, like every morning after you brush your teeth.

ThE BiG "S"

Q "I've been reading about this thing in the news called the 'morning-after pill.' Is it like having an abortion? How does it work?"

A If a woman has unprotected intercourse (like, if the condom broke or if she's been raped), she can take the "morning-after pill" to prevent pregnancy. But let's be clear: The morning-after pill (also known as Emergency Contraception, or E.C.) is not necessarily a Get Out of Pregnancy Free card. It gives you a last chance to avoid getting pregnant, but one in four women who take it will still get pregnant, and it may keep you in bed for the entire day because it can make you feel like you have the flu, or make you throw up. E.C. pills contain high doses of estrogen and progesterone, or just progesterone, which can stop or delay ovulation. That way, there's no egg for the sperm to fertilize (this is not an abortion). If there's an already-fertilized egg, E.C. may prevent it from attaching to the uterine wall and growing. For E.C. to work, you'll need to get and fill a prescription for it within 72 hours of having unprotected sex (go to **not-2-late.com** for info on E.C. brands and doctors in your area). Then you have to take two doses 12 hours apart. But instead of finding yourself in need of E.C., protect yourself with two kinds of birth control—a condom (to help prevent STDs) and one other method.

CG! TIP: Check out **iwannaknow.org** to learn about all the contraception options that are available.

condom sense

Q **"Is there any way I can get a disease from someone even if he's wearing a condom?"**

A We hate to say it, but yes. Latex condoms are highly effective in preventing the spread of STDs like HIV, but condoms aren't *completely* safe, because they're not always put on properly, and even if they are, they can break. Also, even if the guy is wearing a condom, his genital area still comes into contact with yours—and herpes and pubic lice can be spread that way. The only sure way to avoid getting an STD is not to have sex at all. But if you are sexually active, it's essential to use a condom because they're still the best available protection from STDs.

CG! TIP: A recent study found that more than half of STD-infected boys don't tell their partners, so be sure to *always* use a condom!

ThE BiG "S"

Q "What are the risks of having sex in water if he's wearing protection?"

A A condom can break more easily, which can lead to pregnancy or an STD. Water washes away the natural lubrication of your vagina. That makes penetration more difficult, so there's a greater chance that the condom will tear. If you're going to have sex in water no matter what we say, at least use spermicidal foam, cream, or VCF film (a tiny square with spermicide that dissolves in your vagina) as backup protection. (And remember, even when you use those, you're still vulnerable to STDs.) Bottom line? Since it's more difficult to use any type of protection in water, and no protection is foolproof as it is, it's just not worth the risk.

Q "My boyfriend and I are having sex and we're using condoms for protection. But it still makes me nervous that something can happen and I can still get pregnant. How can you make sure a condom will work?"

A A condom is almost as effective as the Pill when it's used properly. When it doesn't work, it's usually because something has gone wrong. If the expiration date of the condom has expired, the condom could be dried out. Since moisture keeps the latex durable, a dried out condom could tear easily. If there's any doubt, toss it! A condom could also weaken and tear if you use an oil-based lubricant, like Vaseline, baby oil, Crisco, and even some body lotions. Be sure to tell your boyfriend that his wallet is not the best place to keep a condom. The heat and pressure in a wallet may cause the wrapper to tear, which could dry out the condom and make it more likely to rip. Never use your teeth or scissors to open a condom. Anything sharp could tear the condom itself, so open the wrapper carefully, at the little slash in the corner of the package.

Q "I'm allergic to latex condoms, and I've heard that lambskin condoms aren't reliable. What do I do?"

A Used correctly, lambskin condoms prevent pregnancy 98 percent of the time, but they're totally ineffective against sexually transmitted diseases. If you are allergic to latex, your best defense is polyurethane—a type of material that stops sperm and the transmission of STDs. (There's a brand called Avanti you can find at most drugstores.) But remember, for 100 percent safe sex protection, hold off on having sexual intercourse altogether.

ThE BiG "S"

pregnant pause

Q **"My boyfriend and I were fooling around, and he touched himself and put the same fingers inside me. Can I get pregnant?"**

A It's very unlikely but not impossible. He would have had to touch himself while semen or pre-ejaculatory fluid was on his penis. Then he would have had to carry some of this fluid on his hand into your vagina. Until the fluid dries, the sperm in it may still be alive. If getting pregnant is not just an option, the safest thing to do is to make him wear a condom even if you're not actually having intercourse (it's the only sure way!).

Q **"I've heard that if you have sex while you are on your period, you can't get pregnant. Is that true or is it just a myth?"**

A It's a total myth! Your menstrual cycle can be very irregular during the first few years of getting your period. As a result, the days you ovulate (when an egg is released from your ovaries and is ready for fertilization) may vary each month. Sperm can actually live inside you for seven days, so if you have unprotected sex while you have your period and your cycle is short that month, your partner's sperm could still be alive when you ovulate—and you could get pregnant. Also, as your body adjusts to hormones during your cycle, fluctuations can cause you to "spot"—you may see some blood in your underwear and think it's your period when it's not. The bottom line? Just because you see blood doesn't mean you're not fertile at the time.

CG! TIP: Unprotected sex always puts you at risk for pregnancy and STDs.

Q **"My boyfriend and I are sexually active, and just two days ago, the condom broke. I'm not sure that I'm pregnant, but what are the odds that I'm not?"**

A About 33 percent of women who have unprotected sex just once end up pregnant, according to Planned Parenthood. So the important question you need to answer right now is, are you pregnant? If you decide you really can't talk to your mom or another adult you trust, call 800-230-7526 to find a clinic near you. Bring your boyfriend along for moral support—don't be afraid to tell him. Just say that since the condom broke, you want to make sure there won't be any surprises. (If you don't bring him, bring your best friend.) Go to a doctor or a clinic instead of taking a test at home because if you are pregnant, you'll have someone there who's trained to discuss your options. Whenever you go, find out about backup birth control (you should always use two forms of birth control). You can ask about Emergency Contraception (E.C.), which, if taken within 72 hours of an "accident," can stop or delay ovulation so you won't get pregnant (see page 110). But remember, if you're sexually active, accidents like this can happen.

> **CG! TIP:** Even if you practice safe sex, something might not work properly and you could get pregnant. Be sure you're ready to take that risk before you have sex.

Q "I've been having sex with my boyfriend for a few months now, and I'm scared that this month I may be pregnant. What are the signs of pregnancy?"

A A missed period is the most common sign, but if you have irregular cycles (you skip months), it's not the most reliable sign for you. A lot of the early signs feel like PMS—tender, swollen breasts, headaches, backaches, or feeling extreme tiredness. If your areola (the nipple area) gets darker brown than usual, that could also be an early sign. Also, many women feel nauseated (they call it morning sickness, but it can happen any time of day) and urinate a lot. The only way to know for sure, though, is from a urine or blood test. You can get one from a doctor or a clinic (or do an at-home test—it's as effective, if done correctly) two weeks after you've missed your period. Most Planned Parenthood clinics have hours for walk-in pregnancy testing (some right after school), and the cost is based on what you can afford. The service is completely confidential, so if you don't want your parents to find out, they won't. If it turns out you are pregnant, talk to an adult you trust about what to do next. If you don't feel like you have an adult to confide in, discuss your options with a counselor at a clinic. If you're scared to go alone, bring a friend.

gyno-anxiety

Q "I'm sixteen years old and I've been thinking it might be time I started to see a gynecologist. So how do I find a good one?"

A If your mom's in the loop, you can always ask her to set up an appointment for you with her gynecologist or you can ask friends to recommend a doctor she likes. But keep in mind, you don't have to go to a gyno to get your first gynecological exam. If you feel more comfortable going to a doctor you know, ask your family physician—many pediatricians are willing to perform these types of exams on their teen patients. It's best to get your parents' help when it comes to the gyno, but if you're going to go on your own, try Planned Parenthood—they offer gynecological exams at reduced rates (and you don't need your parents' permission to get an appointment). To find a clinic near you, call 800-230-7526 or go to **plannedparenthood.org** on the Web for more information.

ThE BiG "S"

Q "I'm going to see my gynecologist for the first time since I lost my virginity last month. Will she know that I've had sex?"

A She'll probably suspect it because in a routine exam, she'll notice that your hymen is broken or stretched. (But remember, that can also happen from using tampons and riding a bicycle.) But, hey, if you are sexually active, you should *want* your gyno to know. She can screen you for STDs, prescribe birth control if you need it, and answer any other sex questions you have. But know that confidentiality laws vary from state to state—some states, for instance, require your doctor to notify your parents if you're having an abortion. So ask your doc what the laws are in your state *before* the exam.

CG! TIP: Whether you go to a female or male gynecologist is really up to you. It's whatever you're most comfortable with.

Q "Do I have to request tests for HIV and other STDs—or will my gyno just do them?"

A It's important to talk to your doctor about your sexual experiences. And if you're worried about AIDS, say so! That way, she can do all the tests you need for good health and peace of mind.

Q "I want to go on the Pill, but I absolutely hate going to the gyno. Is there a legal way for me to get birth control pills without an exam?"

A At some clinics, you can get a Pill prescription without a pelvic exam—at least initially. But an exam is a good idea if you're sexually active so your doctor can check you for STDs. Planned Parenthood offers confidential contraception services and counseling in all 50 states.

CG! TIP: Going to the gyno might freak you out but just remember this: every woman goes, we all survive it, and it's all over in about five minutes!

ChAPTeR 5

serious issues

Sometimes the stuff that goes on in our bodies *is* more serious—and those things call for more serious advice. Here are some of the heavier topics that CosmoGIRL!s have had to tackle, and how you can deal with them too—if you ever need to.

stds

Q "My PAP smear showed I have HPV, but I've never had an outbreak of genital warts. I'm afraid to tell my boyfriend. Do I have to?"

A HPV is the name of a large family of viruses that includes genital warts (painless cauliflower-like bumps on your genitals), as well as other strains that can cause cervical cancer. So it's possible to test positive for HPV and not have genital warts. Either way, you do have to tell your boyfriend (sorry!), because you can transmit the virus to him through skin-to-skin contact or bodily fluids. That's why, if you're sexually active, using condoms is even more important now—they're the best way to make sure that you won't pass it on. It'll be hard to tell him, but if the situation were reversed, wouldn't you want him to be honest with you? Start by telling him exactly what you've told us, then tell him that condoms should protect him, but they aren't a 100 percent guarantee. HPV is not the end of the world. And if you don't make it sound like it is, he may not think it is, either. If he wants more information, tell him to check out **ashastd.org**.

Q "I'm worried I may have passed Chlamydia to two other people. How do I tell them?"

A When you tell a guy you've been with that you have an STD, give it to him straight (hard as it will be, you must for his own protection). Say that you were diagnosed with Chlamydia, and since you were together, he should get tested too. If he gets angry, tell him you understand, but you're concerned about him and the important thing is for him to get tested. After all, Chlamydia strikes 1 out of every 10 teens. The disease is nicknamed "the great masquerader" because it is often symptom-free, but if left untreated, it could hurt your ability to become pregnant in the future.

Q "I've heard that cold sores and herpes caused by the same virus. Is this true?"

A Yes. That means a guy with oral or genital herpes can give you both types of the disease. In other words, His mouth could infect your genitals and vice versa. An outbreak goes like this: (1) Tingling. (2) Blister. (3) Blister oozes. (4) Crust forms. (5) Crust falls off. You can catch or spread herpes during all these phases, so don't fool around!

CG! TIP: A cold sore can be contagious even before it hits the surface. If you get that knowing tingle, steer clear of contact!

SeRiOuS IsSuEs

Q **"If I just fool around with my boyfriend but don't actually have sex, can I catch an STD if he has one?"**

A Fooling around, or hooking up without actually having sexual intercourse, is *safer* than having regular sex—but that doesn't mean it's *safe*. It's difficult but not impossible to get Chlamydia, gonorrhea, and HIV from giving and receiving oral sex. You can get HPV (warts) from giving him oral sex and by grinding genitals, and Hepatitis B from French kissing, touching his genitals, and giving him oral sex. And the two easiest STDs to get? Syphilis and Herpes. You can get each of these from French kissing, touching his genitals, giving and receiving oral sex, and grinding genitals. Remember: The only way to be truly safe from contracting an STD is to not have sex—in any way!

Q **"Before you have sex, should you tell him if you have an STD?"**

A As hard as it may be to do, the answer is yes. Half the new cases of STDs in the U.S. are among 15- to 24-year-olds. So it's imperative that you prevent them from spreading even further by being honest with your partner. You may have an STD, but by being honest, you and he can both discuss what steps to take to protect yourselves. If he wants to break up, then be glad you found out *before* you slept with him. You want a guy who'll love you *more* for being honest. And believe us, there are a lot of guys who will.

CG! TIP: Visit **teenhealth.org** to get all kinds of information on teen health issues.

Q "I found a prescription of my mom's that she said was for vitamins, but I looked the name up on the Web and learned it's for her herpes! I don't know why my mother wouldn't tell me the truth. I can't be mad at her forever, but I also can't act like I don't know. Help!"

A A lot of people would not be able to get past the herpes news itself, so kudos to you for your maturity! You're focusing on the real difficulty: the fact that your mom wasn't honest with you. And you have *every* right to be upset. But also keep in mind that your mom may *really* be taking the prescription for a purpose other than herpes. Lots of medications have multiple uses. If your mom does have herpes, it could be something she's been dealing with for years, and when you were younger, it wouldn't have been appropriate for her to tell you because you wouldn't have understood. Even though you're older now, she may not feel comfortable talking about it with you. Or maybe she never meant to mislead you, but you caught her off guard and she got flustered. *Whatever* her reason for trying to cover it up, you need to approach your mom—calmly—and tell her you feel hurt. Tell her you'd rather she be honest, even if she's looking out for your best interests. But remember to respect her privacy; people who are close do not *have* to tell each other everything. So hear her out, and respect her wishes. Come up with an agreement where you can both use "I don't feel comfortable talking to you about that" whenever you want to keep your privacy. That way, you'll know each other's boundaries, and neither of you will feel like you have to lie.

SeRiOuS IsSuEs

Q "My mom has genital herpes. Can I get it if I touch her underwear?"

A Herpes is a virus that causes blister-like sores in the mouth and on the genitals. It's most contagious during an outbreak, but it can be passed by an infected person at any time. Since it's not airborne, you won't get it from touching your mom's clothes or sitting on the toilet after she has. It's unlikely that you'll catch genital herpes from anyone without direct contact with their genitals. The only way you could catch it from your mom is if you wore her underwear immediately after she did without washing it. Not likely, right?

CG! TIP: Moms are human—just like you—and are entitled to their privacy. You don't tell your mom everything you do, so you can't expect her to tell you everything, too.

Q "I read somewhere that you can get HIV from 'bodily fluids.' Can you get it from French kissing?"

A It's true that you can get HIV from bodily fluids, though some are more difficult to get it from than others. HIV is transmitted when blood, semen (including preseminal fluids which are released before a guy ejaculates), vaginal fluid, saliva, or breast milk from an infected person enters your body. French kissing is considered "low-risk," though saliva does have low levels of HIV, which can enter an uninfected person's body if she has open cuts or sores in her mouth. You're smart to be concerned about HIV— about half of all new HIV infections are among people ages 15 to 25. Before becoming sexually active with anyone, ask about his or her health status and sexual history. If they've been sexually active but haven't had an HIV-test, or they won't even talk about it, hold off on getting physical. Your safety comes first!

CG! TIP: To learn more about HIV, go to **ashastd.org.**

friends in trouble

Q **"I think my friend may be a druggie. Help!"**

A If you think you or a friend may be developing a problem with drugs or alcohol, get help *now.* Things can get out of control fast: Talk to your parents—or get help confidentially at the National Council on Alcohol and Drug Dependence (**www.ncadd.org**) by calling 800-NCA-CALL or 800-475-HOPE. Or check out Narcotics Anonymous (**na.org**) or Alcoholics Anonymous (**alcoholics-anonymous.org**) for support group meetings near you. And in case of an overdose, call 911 or the National Poison Control Center (800-222-1222) immediately.

SeRiOuS IsSuEs

Q: "I think my friend is pregnant, but she won't admit it. What should I do?"

A If you think your friend is pregnant, approach her about it casually. If she isn't ready to face her pregnancy, she may get defensive if you just ask "Are you pregnant?" Try asking if she's all right. If something's really wrong, she'll either tell you or you'll see it on her face. Be direct if being indirect doesn't work. But ask her calmly, not accusingly. If she is pregnant, let her know that you're there for her and offer to go with her to talk to an adult or counselor. If she still refuses to discuss it, get an adult involved. If you feel more comfortable approaching someone you know about this (like your mom or school's guidance counselor) do so. But if you don't, try contacting Project Cuddle at **projectcuddle.org** (888-628-3353) or Planned Parenthood at **plannedparenthood.org** (800-230-7526). Remember, your friend might be angry with you at first, but her health (and her baby's) is worth taking that risk.

Q **"A good friend recently told me she is four months pregnant and is having the baby. I was so shocked that she hadn't told me sooner—and so angry that she was wasting her life—that I stopped talking to her. Now I regret it. What should I do?"**

A We can only *imagine* how scared your friend was when she got the news. Like a lot of women, she may not even have been sure she was pregnant until two months into the pregnancy; then she probably needed time to let the news sink in. So four months isn't exactly *that* long to wait—especially because, since she knows you, she might have predicted that you'd disapprove and was scared to hear what you'd say. But the issue isn't when she told you, it's that she told you at all— that she hoped for your support. So although rejecting her wasn't right (turning your back on a friend never is), you *can* still make things better. First, call her and say, "I'm so sorry if I hurt you. I was shocked, but I *really* want to be there for you." Ask how you can help her when she has the baby: Does she need a babysitter while she gets a haircut? An extra set of hands for food shopping? Those are little ways you can be a *huge* help to her. You might also want to visit **morningglorypress.com** for teen parenting books or call Planned Parenthood for her to find local resources for teen moms. With a child in her life, your friend's world will continue to change in big ways almost every day. Let your friendship with her be at least one thing she'll know she can count on for sure.

> **CG! TIP:** Being a pregnant teen is a scary thing. The best thing you can do for a friend who's pregnant is to be her friend, plain and simple.

SeRiOuS IsSuEs

Q **"I have a serious problem with one of my friends: She told one of our other friends that she thinks about committing suicide, and made her promise not to tell anyone at all! Our friend was scared, so she came to me for help. But what can I do?"**

A If you're concerned a friend may be considering taking her own life, ask her point-blank if she's ever thought about suicide. Contrary to what you might think, asking someone if they've thought about suicide will not put ideas in her head. If she says that she does feel depressed, anxious, or suicidal, talk to an adult you trust (like a guidance counselor or teacher) right away. Even if she asks you to keep her suicidal feelings a secret, don't! It's a myth that people who talk about suicide don't do it. In fact, people who talk about it are at greater risk. Research also shows that often a depressed or suicidal teenager will confide in only one friend—so if you think someone's in trouble, it's very important for you to speak up. Don't wait for someone else to. If you don't feel comfortable talking to any adults you know, call the 24-hour National Youth Crisis Helpline at 800-SUICIDE. Also check out the site **yellowribbon.org**. It was created by the parents of a teen who killed himself. You can download yellow cards to give to friends. The idea is that if they're too embarrassed to ask for help, they can just hand the card to an adult and the cards will tell the adult how to help.

heredity issues

Q **"My aunt Irene and my grandfather both had skin cancer. I have light skin and have always been a sun worshipper. Now I'm really scared that I'll get it. Am I overreacting?"**

A The good news is that skin cancer is one of the most avoidable cancers. The bad news is that most people don't take the right precautions—or any precautions—to avoid it. Skin cancer develops when ultraviolet rays from the sun or a tanning bed heat your skin and damage the cells, causing them to mutate. Skin can get sun damage from everyday exposure, even through windows. People who have moles are more likely to get it. But that doesn't mean it's a sure thing. Always wear SPF 15 on your face and lips. The hottest summer sun can burn your skin in just minutes. So apply an SPF 30 or higher 30 minutes before you hang out outside. Even the highest SPF does not give you 100 percent protection, so wear a hat and get into the shade whenever you can. Too much sun damage, especially before the age of 18, can cause melanoma, the deadliest skin cancer. So stay out of the sun (unless you're well protected)! If you're really worried, see a dermatologist, especially if you have light skin with lots of freckles and moles. Your dermatologist can remove moles before they become problematic. If a mole becomes itchy or scabby, or changes appearance, make an appointment as soon as possible. It may be nothing, but getting checked means you'll know for sure!

SeRiOuS IsSuEs

Q **"What exactly is diabetes? Is it possible to actually die from it?"**

A Diabetes is a lifelong condition in which the body either doesn't produce or properly use insulin (a hormone that helps turn food into energy). Without insulin, sugar builds up in the blood. This is called high blood sugar, and causes symptoms like intense thirst, fatigue, and the need to pee often. But it's the possible long-term effects of high blood sugar—kidney failure, stroke, blindness—that can make it a serious, even fatal, problem. If left untreated, you could go into a diabetic coma and die, but that's rare.

There are two kinds of diabetes: *Type I diabetes* means your body (specifically your pancreas) can't make enough insulin. Doctors aren't sure why some people's systems stop making insulin, but the biggest risk factor seems to be genetics. (Type I is often passed down through your family.) It's most common among kids and teens, but it *can* strike people at any age. To keep blood-sugar levels normal, Type I diabetics have to inject themselves with insulin several times a day and eat a healthy diet limiting sweets to prevent their blood-sugar levels from getting too high.

Type II diabetes is much more common. With this type, the body has grown resistant to insulin and no longer uses it correctly. Obesity is the greatest risk factor. (Being overweight makes your body tissue less sensitive to insulin.) Type II *used* to affect mainly older, overweight adults. But in the past 10 years, cases in young adults have shot up since rates of teen obesity have *also* skyrocketed. Remember, diabetes doesn't have to be a scary thing. By keeping your weight down, getting lots of exercise, and taking medication, it can be controlled.

CG! TIP: Diabetes is easy to control, and most diabetics live normal, healthy lives.

Q "Is there anything you can do to prevent heart disease and depression if they run in your family?"

A If heart disease or depression run in your family—meaning a parent or other relative has had it—that doesn't mean you'll automatically get it. But the genetic link is a factor you shouldn't ignore. Family history can increase your odds of getting heart disease by about 50 percent, and having a parent with depression ups your risk factor for that illness at least threefold. But there's plenty you can do now to head off these problems. Don't smoke. Smoking can cause heart disease as well as cancer. Women who die of a smoking-related disease shave 14.5 years off their lives. Eat right. People who load up on fruits, vegetables, whole grains, and low-fat dairy products—while staying away from greasy foods like burgers and fries—cut their risk of heart disease by avoiding obesity. Research suggests that eating foods like whole grain breads and cereals also may help prevent dips in the brain chemical serotonin, which can lead to depression. Exercise regularly. Working out keeps you in shape so you are less likely to become overweight, a major risk factor for heart disease. It also boots the feel-good brain chemicals called endorphins. Don't drink. Heavy drinking is tied to heart disease because it can raise blood pressure and lead to obesity. But just as damaging are the sudden mood swings drinking can cause, which can trigger depression and other mental illnesses that may run in your family. If you know a disease runs in your family, tell your doctor. She can watch for symptoms.

smoke out

Q "I'm thinking about starting smoking, but I hear it's really bad for you. But so many people smoke—can it really be that bad for you?"

A Yes, yes, yes! If you don't smoke now, please, please, please don't start. Don't think it's all that bad for you? Then you haven't done your homework. In the United States alone, 38,000 people die each year from diseases caused by secondhand smoke. Also, 57 percent more women will die of lung cancer than of breast cancer this year. And why is it never a good time to start? Seventh graders who smoke are 21 percent more likely to go on to smoke pot and 36 times more likely to do hard drugs. On top of that, smoking burns your throat, it makes your clothes and hair smell bad, and it can even turn your fingers yellow. What's cool about that?

CG! TIP: If you light up because you're bored, do something else instead. When you get the urge to smoke, break out your sketchbook, make a batch of cookies, or do something else you enjoy!

Q "I started to smoke about a year and a half ago. When I go to my doctor for my checkup, will she be able to tell?"

A It depends. Smoking can cause you to develop symptoms that a doctor might notice during a routine checkup, such as a chronic cough, irritation of your throat and vocal cords, shortness of breath, or high blood pressure. If your doctor notices these things, she might ask you if you smoke. Even if she doesn't notice these symptoms, most doctors will ask you general questions about your health during an exam, including whether or not you smoke. If she does ask that question, you should tell the truth so she can make the appropriate recommendations for your care (for example, certain medications should not be combined with smoking). Not to lecture you, but: Smoking kills! So while you're at the doctor, ask her about your options for help with quitting. If you stop now, you can still undo any damage to your lungs and heart, which will greatly lower your risk of cancer and heart disease down the road.

SeRiOuS IsSuEs

Q "I smoke and I'm trying to quit. But it's so hard! What should I do?"

A It may be hard to kick the habit, but you've already taken a very important step—you've decided you have to give it up! Good for you! If quitting cold turkey seems like it will be too hard to do, don't worry. There are many other options. Consider joining a cessation program. The support of others helps lots of people kick the habit. Call the American Cancer Society at 800-ACS-2345 to find programs in your area. You could also try nicotine replacements, which help control your urge for nicotine by giving you progressively smaller doses. Available at drugstores and by prescription, they come in many forms—gum, the patch, and lozenges. Doctors can also prescribe nicotine-free bupropion (Zyban) to smokers (even teens) to help control their urge to light up. Get more information at **tobaccofree.com**. Some former smokers have benefited from alternative techniques, like hypnosis and acupuncture, but there is no scientific proof that these work.

CG! TIP: If you smoke, brush your teeth after every meal. It will turn you off your post-meal nicotine cravings.

breast distress

Q **"If I get breast implants, will I be able to breast-feed when I get older?"**

A The short answer is yes. But remember, your breasts grow until you're 18, or even older. So right now, you don't know how big you'll ultimately be! Once your breasts *have* stopped growing, if you still want implants, make sure you find a board-certified surgeon and tell her your concerns about breast-feeding. She should agree to make the incision *under* the armpit or breast or on the borders of your nipples, which should avoid damage to the milk ducts.

Q **"Help me—I'm so scared... I have lumps in my breasts. Do you think I could have cancer? I'm only fifteen years old!"**

A Okay, take a breath and relax a little: Because of your age, it's very unlikely that you do have breast cancer. But it's not impossible, which means you should be cautious and definitely get yourself checked out, especially if there's a history of breast cancer in your family. In 2004, about 216,000 women were diagnosed with breast cancer, and about 40,000 died from the disease. But if the cancer is detected in time to be treated, a woman can survive.

SeRiOuS IsSuEs

That's why getting to know your breasts and all their *normal* lumps (which are just tissue or fluid or both) is crucial. Most doctors recommend that all girls start giving themselves monthly self-exams after age 20, but there's no reason you shouldn't start *now*.

Q **"One of my nipples is tucked in. I read this could be a sign of cancer. Is this true? Breast cancer runs in my family!"**

A Your innie nipple is probably not a sign of cancer, but given your family history, it would be smart to have a doctor take a look. Most likely, you're part of the 10 percent of women who have inverted nipples. This happens when the connective tissues that run from the center of your breasts to your milk ducts—located underneath your nipples—are slightly short. That nipple might still pop out if your breast tissue grows, which can sometimes happen during pregnancy.

CG! TIP: Visit **breastcancer.org** for a lesson on how to do a breast self-exam (BSE) and for information about how to prevent breast cancer.

gastric bypass surgery

Q **"I am overweight and have tried unsuccessfully for years to lose weight. Should I consider gastric bypass surgery?"**

A Gastric bypass surgery is a controversial procedure that reduces the size of your stomach from a football to an egg. Risks include nutritional deficiencies like anemia and osteoporosis, malnutrition, and gallstones. For these reasons especially, not everyone is given the option to have gastric bypass surgery. It might be viable for you. For the most part, candidates for this type of surgery must have a Body Mass Index-for-age in the ninety-fifth percentile (see **cdc.gov/nchs/about/major/nhanes/ growthcharts/ clinical_charts.htm**) and a life-threatening obesity-related health problem like diabetes, severe sleep apnea, or heart disease. If you are eligible for the surgery, however, know what you're getting into. Head to **asbs.org** to get more information.

CG! TIP: Graze like a cow to keep your energy up throughout the day. Go from eating three big meals a day to five mini-meals.

sexual identity

Q **"I've been noticing the girls more than the boys in X-rated movies lately. Do you think I might be gay?"**

A Noticing girls in a movie or even in a fantasy or dream doesn't mean you're a lesbian. Obviously, in some cases, focusing on members of the same sex does develop into a strong attraction to real-life women, like friends or even teachers. More likely, you're just getting in touch with your own sense of femaleness—but the place to do that is not in front of a TV watching X-rated movies. Porno films can give you the wrong idea of what sexual relationships are all about, no matter which gender you focus on.

CG! TIP: If you're confused about your sexuality and want to get some help working it out, you can call the Gay and Lesbian National Hotline, toll-free, at 888-THE-GLNH.

InDeX

InDeX

InDeX